CONTRIBUTIONS TO STATISTICAL

ANALYSIS :

SENSIBILITY (STABILITY AND CONSISTENCY) OF SEVERAL COEFFICIENTS OF RELATIVE VARIANCE AND THE COEFFICIENT OF PROPORTIONAL VARIANCE (Cpv)

THE COEFFICIENT OF CONTENT VALIDITY (Ccv) AND THE KAPPA COEFFICIENT (K) IN THE DETERMINATION OF CONTENT VALIDITY, USING THE TECHNIQUE OF "PANEL OF EXPERTS"

Rafael A. Hernández Nieto, M. Sc., Ph. D.

Master of Science in Education
(University of Wisconsin, USA)
Ph. D. Research Methodology in Mathematics Education
(Quantitative Methods)
(University of Wisconsin, USA)
Graduate Courses in Biostatistics and Clinical
Epidemiology
(John Hopkins University, Baltimore, USA)
Post-doctorate in Computer Science Applied to the
Teaching of Mathematics
(University of Iowa and University of Wisconsin, USA)

Full Professor in Applied Statistics, Research Methodology and Computer Science. School of Education
Former - Coordinator and Founder of the Master´s Degree Program in Computer Education and Instructional Design, School of Education

General Coordinator of Computer Science. Law, Political and Criminology Sciences School

Professor of Biostatistics, Master´s Degree Program in Toxicology
Professor of Biostatistics, Master´s Degree Program in Microbiology
Professor of Biostatistics, Master´s Degree Program in Immunology
Professor of Research Methodology, Master´s Degree Program in Political Sciences

Professor of Statistics, Graduate Program in Agrarian Development

Universidad de Los Andes
Mérida, Venezuela - July 2002

Author:

Ⓔ **Rafael Hernández Nieto, M.Sc., Ph. D., 2002**

Ⓔ **Design (front and back cover, text and graphics): Rafael**

Hernández Nieto, M.Sc., Ph. D., 2002

Coedited by:

UNIVERSIDAD DE LOS ANDES

Facultad de Ciencias Jurídicas, Políticas y Criminológicas
Coordinación General de Informática
Laboratorio de Docencia e Investigación
Mérida, Venezuela

INSTITUTO DE ESTUDIOS EN INFORMÁTICA
Servicios Profesionales en Informática y Estadística- Entrenamiento-Consultorías
Soporte en Redes Linux
Centro Comercial "Alto Chama" – Torre Norte – Piso 3 – Oficina TN3-03
Telefax: (0274) 271-1284 – Correo Electrónico: iesinfo2001@yahoo.com
La Parroquia – Mérida, Venezuela

Contributions to Statistical Analysis
©Rafael Hernández-Nieto, Ph. D.

ISBN: 158-898-715-9

Legal Deposit: lf 074 2001 0012 141

First Edition

Mérida, Venezuela
July, 2002

DEDICATORY:

To my father:

> **Antonio María**

To my mother:

> **Ana Graciela**

To my wife:

> **Rubia Teresita**

To my sons: **Lenin Alberto, Katyuska Sophía, Rafael Alberto, Ninotska Graciela Helí Antonio**

To my granchildren: Lenín Andrés, Herfrank Elí, Martín Santiago, Manuela, Camila de Fátima, Juan David, Diego Rafael

FOREWORD

Within the every day routine of the university academic life of teaching and doing research, some personal experiences emerge, which can not be found in books, and which are very important and useful to university students; I believe that is the case of Professor Rafael Hernández Nieto, who has been able to develop two new instruments for statistical analysis, which I am sure will help university students in their process of learning statistics, a subject matter somewhat difficult to understand because of the very nature of its content.

From an statistical point of view, the development of a coefficient requires of perseverance in the thoughtness on the subject under study,   until *suddenly*, by means which are not clearly defined within the psychological processes involved, the new idea, the CREATIVE ONE irrupts (some people even call this process a "divine intervention") to offer some answers to the problems of science (in this case statistics) and, at the same time, making contributions for the advancement in the teaching of this science.

In this work, two new coefficients have been proposed: the ***Coefficient of Proportional Variance (Cpv)*** and the ***Coefficient of Content Validity (Ccv)***. The *Coefficient of Proportional Variance* proposes a solution to the problem of measuring and evaluating the *relative variability* of a given distribution, obviating the problems of subjective interpretation and value judgments. The mathematical relationship derived from the ***Cpv*** allows for a more precise and more scientific interpretation of relative variability of data.

The *Coefficient of Content Validity* permits the calculation of the content validity for each item, as well as the total content validity, of any data collection instrument that has been subjected to the evaluation of several judges (Panel of Experts Technique). Until now, according to the psychometric and statistical literature, a *quantitative estimator* of the content validity of a measuring instrument had not been achieved.

I am certain that these two research works from Professor Hernández-Nieto, constitute an important contribution to the field that will facilitate a better understanding and interpretation of data variability and measurement validity, mainly in the area of the Social Sciences, but also in the general area of Applied Statistics. These new instruments will serve as material of necessary support and reference not only for students but also for researchers using statistics.

Prof. Mariano J. Durán N., M. Sc.,
"Doctoral Candidate" in Biometrics
(Syracuse University, N. Y.)

Professor of Statistics and Biometrics
Department of Forestry and Environmental Sciences
Universidad de Los Andes

Mérida, Venezuela – 2002

GENERAL CONTENT

ACKNOWLEDGEMENTS

To Professors Thomas A. Romberg and Gary A. Price, of the University of Wisconsin (Madison, Wisconsin), from whom I learned the fundamental principles of quantitative research methodology at the same time of developing in me the love and passion for "doing research".

To Professor Nicolaus Walzuch (deceased), from the Computer Laboratory, School of Engineering, Universidad de los Andes (Mérida, Venezuela), for the first computer program, on the Eclipse Computer S-140, written in 1980, to compute the *Coefficient of Proportional Variance (Cpv)* in different types of distributions.

To my son, Systems Engineer Rafael Alberto Hernández-Urdaneta, for the software written in matrix language of Spss, to calculate the *Kappa Coefficient*, based on the algorithm developed by Fleiss, when the number of objects to be evaluated is larger than 1, also, for the program in Spss matrix language, to calculate the *Coefficient of Content Validity*.

To Mrs. Carmen Cristina Herrera-Garrido, for her ability to untangle the hieroglyphics of the first manuscript of this work.

To my daughter, Ninotska Graciela Hernández de Molina, an Instructor at the Foreign Languages School, Universidad Los Andes (Mérida, Venezuela), for the editing of the manuscript (both the initial Spanish version and the later English version).

To professors Christopher Birkbeck (Research Methodology, School of Criminology), Mariano Durán (Statistics and Biometrics, School of Forestry and Environmental Sciences), Jesús Rafael Jiménez (Biostatistics, School of Medicine), José Montes-Gibuba (Research Methodology, School of Education-Mérida) , Ramón Moreno (Measurement and Evaluation, School of Education- Táchira), Mauro Rivas (Mathematics, School of Education - Mérida), all from the Universidad de Los Andes (Mérida, Venezuela), for their critical comments and suggestions to the manuscript.

To the "*Laboratorio de Computación de Investigación y Docencia*" (Computer Laboratory of Teaching and Research), to the "*Consejo de la Facultad*" (Faculty Council) of the "*Facultad de Ciencias Jurídicas, Políticas y*

Criminológicas" (Faculty of Law, Political and Criminology Sciences), Universidad de Los Andes (Mérida, Venezuela), and to the *"Instituto de Estudios en Informática"* (Institute of Studies in Informatics) (La Parroquia -Mérida,Venezuela) for their institutional support during the process of writing and publishing this book.

ABSTRACT

This is not just another book on statistics. It is a book in which two new contributions to statistical analysis are presented and evaluated:

1. The *Coefficient of Proportional Variance (Cpv)*, which allows for the evaluation of the relative variability of a given set of data, using a percentage scale (0 to 100%). A comparative analysis of the *sensibility (stability and consistency)* of this coefficient is made when compared with other well known coefficients (Coefficient of Variance, Coefficient of Range, Coefficient of Average Deviation, Coefficient of Median Deviation, Coefficient of Quartile Variation). The conclusion is reached that the *Cpv* is the only stable and consistent coefficient among the other coefficients. An earlier version of this coefficient was initially presented by the author in 1984.

2. The *Coefficient of Content Validity (Ccv)*, to measure and to evaluate the content validity of data collection instruments, by means of the technique of *Panel of Experts*. The *Ccv* is then compared with the *Kappa Coefficient*, which measures agreement among judges on a given set of items or objects. This coefficient is an extended and more complete version of the *Coefficient of Proportional Ranks* (Hernández-Nieto, 1984, 1995).

Programs and exercises on the Coefficients *Cpv, Ccv* and *Kappa*, using SPSS, are included.

TABLE OF CONTENTS

PART A :

SENSIBILITY (STABILITY AND CONSISTENCY) OF SEVERAL COEFFICIENTS OF RELATIVE VARIANCE AND THE COEFFICIENT OF PROPORTIONAL VARIANCE (Cpv)

LIST OF TABLES

LIST OF FIGURES

TABLE OF CONTENTS

PART B:

THE COEFFICIENT OF CONTENT VALIDITY (Ccv) AND THE KAPPA COEFFICIENT (K) IN THE DETERMINATION OF CONTENT VALIDITY, USING THE TECHNIQUE OF "PANEL OF EXPERTS"

LIST OF TABLES

LIST OF FIGURES

INTRODUCTION

Measuring and evaluating the central tendency, as well as the variability of a given distribution, constitute very important tasks in descriptive statistical analysis. To measure and to evaluate central tendency, the statistics of Mean, Median and Mode have been developed, while to measure variability or dispersion, the measures of *Range, Absolute Deviation from the Mean and Absolute Deviation from the Median* have been widely used.

These measures specify only the way in which the observations tend to be spread around certain value, as well as the grade of oscillation and *"instability"* that these observations manifest around such "central axis" or specific value. However, each one of those measures has certain limitations and disadvantages, mainly the lack of appropriate mathematical properties. The need arises for the development of some alternative procedures that would allow the evaluation and comparability, descriptively, of the variability of two or more distributions, and, at the same time, to evaluate in a more appropriate and precise form, variability within each of the distributions.

Those who have worked during several years on the teaching of descriptive statistics, have faced in many occasions with the problem of "evaluating" the magnitude of a given value of the Standard Deviation or of the Variance. Beyond an explanation based on the conceptual definition of the Standard Deviation as "the average distance, on linear units, based on each of the observations from the arithmetic Mean" (likewise, the Variance explained as "the average distance, in quadratic units, based on each of the observations from the arithmetic Mean"), it is very difficult to evaluate the magnitude of the observed value. Given this problem, some authors have developed certain coefficients in an effort to measure and to evaluate with more precision the magnitude of a given value of the Standard Deviation or of the Variance. However, *these coefficients present several limitations, mainly the lack of a clear mathematical relationship among the terms, which define them.*

The fundamental purpose of this work is to analyze the properties of **sensitivity** *(consistency and stability)* of a coefficient developed by the author (Hernández-Nieto, 1980). This coefficient allows for the *measurement and evaluation of the magnitude* of a given Standard Deviation on a scale whose maximum value is 1.00 (maximum variability) and the minimum value is 0.00 (null variability), based on a *clearly defined and demonstrated mathematical relationship among the terms of such coefficient.*

In Chapter 1 the problem of interpreting the measures of variability is discussed more deeply, and the main limitations of the conventional coefficients are defined and explained. The contributions of Mosteller and

Rourke are also presented, as well as those of Messick, in the search for new procedures when evaluating variability.

In Chapter 2 the author defines and demonstrates the new ***Coefficient of Proportional Variance (Cpv)*** in its two forms: *Coefficient of Scale Proportional Variance (Cpv$_s$)* and the *Coefficient of Empirical Proportional Variance (Cpv$_e$).*

Chapter 3 presents a comparative analysis of the new coefficient with the conventional coefficients on different prototypes of distributions: distributions with the same empirical range, distributions with unequal empirical ranges, distributions with different but equivalent scale bases, distributions with different and non-equivalent scale bases. A comparison is made among all of the conventional coefficients and the new coefficient, in relation to four prototypes of distributions: two distributions with different bases and equivalent scales, and two distributions with different bases and non-equivalent scales.

Chapter 4 offers a complete discussion on the advantages and limitations of the ***Coefficient of Proportional Variance (Cpv).***

Finally, Chapter 5 presents a summary of the main concepts as well as the corresponding conclusions and recommendations.

CHAPTER 1

THE PROBLEM OF INTERPRETING MEASURES

OF VARIABILITY

When someone reads or writes a technical research report in which *Means and Standard Deviations* are included, he/she faces the problem of interpreting the real meaning of the variability of a given set of data.

By definition, the Standard Deviation, the measure of variability mostly used given its statistical properties, is the average of the distances between each one of the observations or scores and the Arithmetic Mean. In symbolic terms:

$$S'_x = \sqrt{\sum (Xi - Mx)^2 / (n-1)}$$

(unbiased estimate), when n < 30

where $X_i = X_1, X_2, \ldots, X_n$; M_x = Arithmetic

Mean; n = sample size

This measure of variability only indicates the average distance between each one of the values of the random variable and the corresponding arithmetic mean, the mean indicating the observed or non-observed value of the variable around which most of those values are dispersed. Since the *Standard Deviation* (S_x) or the *Variance* (S^2_x) is a score or value average of distances, which implies that some of the values could be at a very short distance from the mean; therefore, it is a difficult to evaluate the meaning of a certain value of $\acute{\sigma}_x$ or $\acute{\sigma}^2_x$, unless an evaluation scale is available as a reference criterion.

Another interpretation problem arises from the property of independence among the *Arithmetic Mean* *(M$_x$)* and the *Variance (S^2_x)*. Because of this independence, two or more distributions may show the same mean and, still, demonstrating totally different variances. In the same way, two or more distributions may have different means and at the same time having the same variance.

In *Figures 1a, 1b, 1c, 1d,* and *1e*, some examples are presented in which the observed independence of the arithmetic mean and the standard deviation are shown graphically. In *example a*, the leptokurtic distribution shows a bigger variability when compared to the leptokurtic distribution (equal means); in *example b*, the triangular distribution shows a smaller variability that the one of the rectangular distribution (the arithmetic means are the same); in *example c*, the bimodal distribution presents a bigger variability than that of the multimode distribution (the arithmetic means are the same); in *example d*, each one of the three leptokurtic distributions demonstrate a different arithmetic mean, but the corresponding variances are the same; finally, in *example*

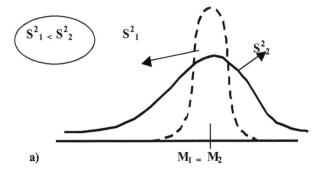

a) $M_1 = M_2$

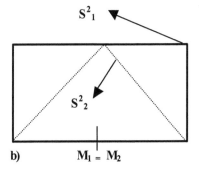

b) $M_1 = M_2$

Figures 1a, 1b:
Independence between the Arithmetic Mean (M_x) and the Variance (S^2_x)

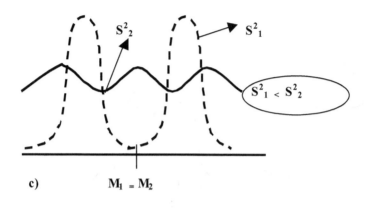

c) $M_1 = M_2$

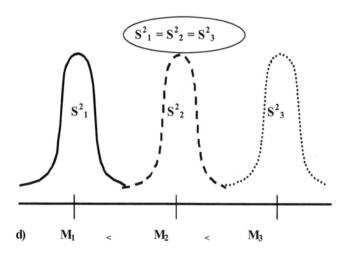

d) M_1 < M_2 < M_3

Figures 1c, 1d:
Independence between the Arithmetic Mean (M_x) and the
Variance (S^2_x)

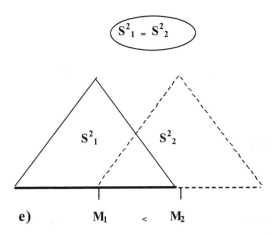

Figure 1e:
Independence between the Arithmetic Mean (M_x)
and the Variance (S^2_x)

e, the two triangular distributions are the same in terms of variability, but their means are different.

Given these considerations, it becomes clear that attaining a meaningful interpretation of the Standard Deviation (or of the Variance) constitutes a real problem. Some questions, such as the following ones, have not been given appropriate and definitive answers:

a) When a single empirical distribution is being evaluated:

a.1. How big or how small is the obtained value of S_x or S^2_x...?

a.2. If the distribution is too asymmetric and / or its kurtosis is too small, does the obtained value of S_x or S^2_x have the same meaning ...

a.3. Which is the existing relationship between the *average distance* around the obtained arithmetic mean (i.e., the Standard Deviation) and the distance between the *maximum observed value* and the *minimum observed value* of the scale *(i.e., the empirical* range) ...?

a.4. Which is the existing relationship between the *average distance* around the obtained arithmetic mean (i.e., the Standard Deviation) and the distance between the *maximum expected value* and the *minimum expected value* of the scale (i.e., the *scale range* or *expected range*) ...?

b) When two or more distributions are being

evaluated:

b.1. How big is the obtained value of Sx or S^2x of a given distribution, when it is compared with the corresponding value of another distribution ...?

b.2. May the same obtained value of S_x or $S^2{}_x$, in two or more distributions, have the same meaning...? Specifically, under the following cases:

b.2.1. Having the same empirical range and different measurement scale (using the same scale base).

b.2.2. Having the same empirical range and different measurement scale (using different scale bases).

b.2.2.1. The measurement scales are different, but they are made equivalent, using certain transformation rule(a linear transformation, for example).

b.2.3. Having *different **empirical ranges*** and the *same **scale range*** (using the same base).

b.2.4. Having *different **empirical ranges*** and *different **scale ranges*** (of the same base).

b.2.5. Having *different **empirical ranges*** and *different **scale ranges*** (using different bases).

In most cases, these problems have been solved by means of value judgments, which may differ significantly from one person to another, and even to differ on the same person from an occasion to another. In some other cases, these problems have been given incomplete solutions, by means of certain coefficients well known. A brief discussion of these coefficients would indicate their main limitations:

Solutions already proposed: the Conventional Coefficients of Relative Variability

After reviewing the   statistical literature, we have found the following ***Conventional Coefficients of Relative Variability***:

1. - ***Coefficient of Variance* or *Coefficient of Relative Variance (CV)***. It is the most widely known coefficient, defined by Garret (1976, p.78) as the "percentage of S_x in relation to the Arithmetic Mean":

$$CV = \left(\frac{Sx}{Mx} \right) x100$$

This coefficient is very useful when two or more distributions are compared on different scales, each one of them expressed on a ratio or quotient scale. However, it is a very unstable and difficult to interpret it, especially when the means of two or more distributions are not the same and the measure scale is at the interval level. Garret, in 1926, already indicated the main problem of this coefficient, using this example:

> *Let us suppose that we have administered a vocabulary test to a group of students, obtaining a mean of 25.00 and a Standard Deviation of 20.00. Then we add to the instrument 10 very easy items. It is expected that all the students know the added words. Therefore, the Mean will be increased in 10 points, while the Standard Deviation will remain the same. An increment of the Mean of 25 to 35 points*

does not correspond with any increment in

Sx neither with a fall of the CV from 20 to

14 points; and since could have added 20

*or 200 items to the test, **the CV is clearly a***

***very unstable statistic.** (p. 59).*

(underlining added).

2. - *Coefficient of Range (CR).* A measure
of variability not frequently used, defined by Shao
(1972, p, 236) as the quotient of the range or width
and the sum, divided by two, of the minimum and
maximum observed scores:

$$CR = \frac{range}{(\min imum + \max imum)/2}$$

In other words, it is the ratio between the empirical range and the midpoint of the same empirical range. The mathematical or statistical properties of this coefficient have not been well defined; therefore, the corresponding computed value is very difficult to interpret. Furthermore, this coefficient may result on a value bigger than one, indicating that it does not represent a true relative variability measure.

3. - *Coefficient of Mean Deviation (CMD)*

Defined as the ratio between the Mean Absolute Deviation (MAD) and the Arithmetic

Mean (Mx) (for symmetrical distributions), according to García-Hoz and Martin-Ferrer (1966):

CMD = Mean Absolute Deviation / Mean

$$CMD = \left[\frac{\sum |Xi - Mx|}{n} \right] (Mx)$$

Given its analogy with CV, we could indicate the same limitations: the mathematical or statistical properties of this coefficient are not well known.

4.- ***Coefficient of Median Deviation (CMDND).*** García-Hoz y Martín-Ferrer (1966), define it as the ratio between the Absolute Median Deviation (AMD) and the Median (Mdn) (for asymmetrical distributions):

$$CMDND = AMD / Mdn$$

$$CMDND = \left[\frac{\sum |Xi - Mdn|}{n} \right] \left(\frac{1}{Mdn} \right)$$

Given the analogy of the **CMED** and the **CMDND** to the **CV**, the same type of limitations should apply: the mathematical properties of their corresponding ratios are not well known.

5. - *Coefficient of Quartile Variation (CQV)*

It was developed with the purpose of evaluating the variability of asymmetric distributions (positive or negative asymmetry).

Proposed by Shao (1972), as the ratio between the Quartile Deviation ($Q_3 - Q_1$) and the midpoint between Quartile 1 (Percentile 25) and Quartile 3 (Percentile 75):

$$CQV = \frac{Q_3 - Q_1}{(Q_3 + Q_1)/2}$$

This coefficient has two major limitations:

a) It is only applicable to asymmetric distributions.

b) It only measures the relative variability of 50% of the central part of the distribution, not taking into consideration the variability on the tails of the distribution.

It is evident that all the coefficients described previously present serious limitations, especially, the absence of a clear mathematical or statistical relationship among the components of the defined equations. In consequence, a clear interpretation of their results becomes quite difficult.

Contributions of Mosteller, Rourke and Messick.

In relation to the important problem of estimating in a quick and simple form the absolute variability of a certain distribution, Mosteller and Rourke (1973) developed a "quick and simple" *estimator* of the Standard Deviation in distributions "approximately" normal. Mosteller and Rourke defined this *estimator* as the ratio between the range of the observed scores ("empirical" range) and a "divider factor " (*dn*), which depends on the size of the sample (for n $\leq$ 15 and for 16 $\leq$ n $\leq$ 100). When n = 15, *dn* is calculated as $\sqrt{n}$; for n $\geq$ 16, the specific values of *dn* are obtained from of a table (Table 1). For example, when n = 150, according to the table, *dn* = 5.30. Also, they found a divider *"substitute"*, based on the range, to carry out a contrast "t *substitute[* (when n $\leq$ 100) (Mosteller and Rourke, 1973, pp. 236, 264, 363). However, the authors *did not explain clearly the procedure to obtain dn.*

Messick (1982) developed what he qualifies as *"some cheap tricks"* to make inferences on the

Table 1
Dividers *dn* for the Range, Compared to $\sqrt{n}$ to Estimate the Standard Deviation on a Given Distribution (Mosteller y Rourke, 1973, p. 363).

n	*dn*	$\sqrt{n}$	*div. subs.* *	*n*	*dn*	$\sqrt{n}$
2	1.13	1.41	1.41	110	5.08	10,49
3	1.69	1.73	1.91	120	5.14	10,95
4	2.06	2.00	2.24	130	5.20	11,40
5	2.33	2.24	2.48	140	5.25	11,83
6	2.53	2.45	2.67	*150*	*5.30*	12,25
7	2.80	2.65	2.83	160	5.34	12,65
8	2.85	2.83	2.96	170	5.38	13,04
9	2.97	3.00	3.08	180	5.42	13,42
10	3.08	3.16	3.18	190	5.46	13,78
11	3.17	3.32	3.27	200	5.49	14,14
12	3.26	3.46	3.35	250	5.64	15,81
13	3.34	3.61	3.42	300	5.76	17,32
14	3.41	3.74	3.49	350	5.85	18,71
15	3.47	3.87	3.55	400	5.94	20,00
16	*3.53*	*4.00*	*3.61*	450	6.01	21,21
17	3.59	4.12	3.66	500	6.07	22,36
18	3.64	4.24	3.71	600	6.18	24,49
19	3.69	4.36	3.76	700	6.28	26,46
20	3.73	4.47	3.81	800	6.35	28,28
30	4.09	5.48	4.17	900	6.42	30,00
40	4.32	6.33	4.40	1000	6.48	31,62
50	4.50	7.07	4.57			
60	4.64	7.75	4.71			
70	4.75	8.37	4.84			
80	4.85	8.94	4.94			
90	4.94	9.49	5.02			
100	5.02	10.00	5.08			

A divider is also included per range, to obtain a substitute Standard Deviation for a "t substitute".
* *"div. subs"* gives a better divider than *dn* to find a value of S_e based on the Range for a contrast "*t substitute*" (when n   100)

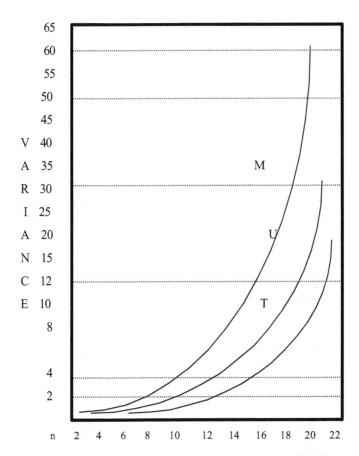

Figure 2:
Variance of Three Prototypes of Random Distributions: Maximum Variance (M), Uniform (U) and Triangular (T), in Function of *n*, the Number of Options (in the case of Items) or Categories (Messick, 1982, p. 753).

form of the distributions; these "tricks" consist of the comparison of the "observed" or empirical variances with the *expected variances* (or maximum variances) of three prototypes of distributions: **bimodal of maximum variance, uniform distribution and triangular distribution** (Messick, 1982, pp. 749 – 758).

To facilitate the comparison between the observed variance and the *expected variance* or *maximum variance*, Messick constructed the corresponding curves of the three prototypes of distributions, according to number of categories/responses on a given scale. For example, on a Likert scale of 7 points (n = 7) the empirical distribution produced a mean of 4 points and a variance of 9.5 points; according to the curve of Figure 2, the *variance* of the **distribution of maximum variance** (bimodal and symmetric, with frequencies equally distributed on each of the two extreme values of the scale), is expected to be 9. This indicates that all the frequencies for each of the extreme answers were equally distributed between 1 and 9. In this case, the mean of 4 does not constitute a good estimator of the central tendency, given the bimodal character of the observed distribution.

However, although the work of Mosteller, Rourke and Messick, made a contribution to the problem of evaluating the *absolute variability* of the three prototypes of distributions, the problem of evaluating *relative variability* was not completely addressed.

CHAPTER 2

A NEW ALTERNATIVE: THE *COEFFICIENT*

OF PROPORTIONAL VARIANCE (Cpv).

DEFINITION AND DEMONSTRATION

This coefficient, developed by the author (Hernández-Nieto, 1980), measures the relative variability of a given group of scores or observations, on the base of a well-defined mathematical relationship between the range (Rx) and the Standard Deviation (Sx). The *Coefficient of Proportional Variance* (*Cpv*) is defined as the ratio between the *observed variability* and the *maximum expected variability*, each one of these variabilities expressed in terms of their corresponding *standard deviations*. Given this relationship, we can define the **Coefficient of Proportional Variance (Cpv)** as the ratio between *two times the Standard Deviation (Sx) and the Range (Rx)*. In symbolic terms:

$$Cpv = 2\,S_x\,/\,R_x$$

where (0.00 ≤ Cpv ≤ 0.00), for N > 30

and

$$Cpv = 2S'_x\,/\,R_x,$$

where (0.00 ≤ Cpv ≤ 1.00), for N ≤ 30 and S'_x is the unbiased estimate of S_x for small samples.

The Distribution of Maximum Variance

Given a bimodal distribution of *maximum variance*, as defined by Messick (1982), where the frequencies (F_i) of the scores are equally distributed among the Minimum score (X_a) and the Maximum score (X_b), such that $F_a = F_b$ (Figure 3), the arithmetic mean is equal to the midpoint of the distance between X_a and X_b.

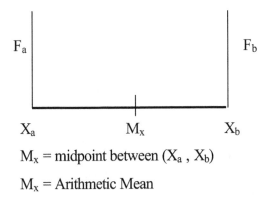

M_x = midpoint between (X_a , X_b)

M_x = Arithmetic Mean

Figure 3. A Bimodal Distribution of Maximum Variability (Messick, 1982, p. 751).

Mean and Standard Deviation of a Maximum Variance Distribution

Arithmetic Mean:

In a distribution of *maximum variance* it can be demonstrated that the Arithmetic Mean is equal to the *midpoint of the distance* between the *maximum score* (X_b) and the *minimum score* (X_a), or range:

$$(1)\ M_x = (X_a + X_b)\ /\ 2$$

The demonstration of (1) can be shown using either/or both of the two equalities that are derived from the distribution of maximum variance: a) the Arithmetic Mean (M_x) is equal to the *minimum score* (X_a) *plus the empirical range* (R_x) *divided by two*. b) the Arithmetic Mean (M_x) is also equal to the *maximum score* (X_b) minus the *empirical range (Rx)* divided by two:

(a) $M_x = X_a + R_x / 2$ **and**

(b) $M_x = X_b - R_x / 2.$

Demonstration of (1), using (a):

$M_x = X_a + R_x / 2$

$M_x = X_a + (X_b - X_a) / 2$

$M_x = (2X_a / 2) + (X_b - X_a) / 2$

$M_x = (2X_a + X_b - X_a) / 2$

$M_x = (X_a + X_b) / 2$

Demonstration of (1), using (b):

$M_x = X_b - R_x / 2$

$M_x = X_b - (X_b - X_a) / 2$

$M_x = (2X_b / 2) - (X_b - X_a) / 2$

$M_x = (X_a + X_b) / 2$

Standard Deviation:

In a distribution of *maximum variance* it can demonstrated that the *Standard Deviation* (S_x) is equal to the absolute value of the distance between the *minimum score* (X_a) and the *Arithmetic Mean* (M_x), or to the *absolute value of the distance* $|d_a|$ between the *maximum score* (X_b) and the *Arithmetic Mean* (M_x):

$$S_x = |d_a| = |X_a - M_x|$$

$$S_x = |d_b| = |X_b - M_x|$$

Where $|d_a| = |d_b|$, since M_x is the midpoint between X_a and X_b.

Equally, it can be demonstrated that the Standard Deviation of a distribution of *maximum variance* is equal to the *Range* divided by two:

$$S_x = (X_b - X_a) / 2 = \textbf{\textit{Range}} / 2$$

Demonstration:

By definition, $S^2{}_x = [F_i (X_i - M_x)^2] / N$ when the data has been organized *using simple frequencies*, not using interval classes; therefore, in a distribution of *maximum variance*:

$$S^2{}_x = [F_1 (X_1 - M_x)^2 + F_2 (X_2 - M_x)^2] / N$$

$$S^2{}_x = [F_a (X_a - M_x)^2 + F_b (X_b - M_x)^2] / N$$

Where:

Fi = simple frequency (for i = 1, 2),

$F_1 = F_a$ to; $F_2 = F_b$; $X_1 = X_a$; $X_2 = X_b$;

$$N = F_1 + F_2$$

$$S^2_x = F \, [(X_a - M_x)^2 + (X_b - M_x)^2] \, / \, 2,$$

since $F_a = F_b = F$

$$S^2_x = F \, (d^2_a + d^2_b) \, / \, N,$$

where $d^2_a = (X_a - M_x)^2$ and $d^2_b = (X_b - M_x)^2$

$$S^2_x = [(N \, / \, 2) \, (2 \, d^2)] \, / \, N,$$

where $d^2_a = d^2_b = d^2$ and $F = N \, / \, 2$

$$S^2_x = (N \, d^2) \, / \, N$$

$S^2_x = d^2$; therefore:

$$\boxed{S_x = |\, d \,|}$$

In a *distribution of maximum variance*, the

Standard Deviation is equal to the absolute distance

between the *maximum score* (X_b) or the *minimum score* (X_a), and the Arithmetic Mean (M_x).

Also, since in this same distribution $(d_a + d_b)$ = range (R_x), $d_a = d_a$ and $S_x = d$, (as it was demonstrated), then:

$$2S_x = R_x$$

That is to say, the *Standard Deviation* is equal to *two times the empirical range*, in a *distribution of maximum variance*.

Therefore, $$S_x = R_x / 2$$

When there is a **null variance** $(S^2_x = 0)$ in the distribution, it becomes obvious that the ***Coefficient*** *of Proportional Variance (Cpv)* is equal to zero, since Sx and Rx are both equal to zero:

$$Cpv = 2\,S_x\,/\,R_x = 2(0)\,/\,0 = 0\,/\,0$$

Thus, by definition, the absence of variability in a given distribution would imply that the corresponding *proportional variance* must be equal to zero, thus, the *Coefficient of Proportional Variance, is equal to zero*. In this case:

$$(X_a - M_x)^2 = 0 \ \ and \ \ (X_b - M_x)^2 = 0$$

since $X_a = X_b = M_x$ (all the values are equal)

In actual data, however, the empirical distribution of a given data set, will oscillate between a *maximum variance (Cpv = 1.00)* and an absolute *absence of variance (Cpv = 0.00)*:

$$0.0 \leq Cpv \leq 1.00$$

Two derived forms of the *Coefficient of Proportional Variance*: the *Coefficient of Empirical Proportional Variance (Cpve)* and the *Coefficient of Scale Proportional Variance (Cpvs).*

The *Coefficient of Proportional Variance (Cpv)* becomes the *Coefficient of Empirical Proportional Variance (Cpv$_e$)* when the distribution includes the values maximum and minimum of the observed scores (empirical or observed range). Also, the *Coefficient of Proportional Variance (Cpv)* becomes the *Coefficient of Scalar Proportional Variance (Cpv$_s$)* when the distribution includes the *maximum* and the *minimum* values (observed or non-observed) of the **measuring scale** being used.

$$Cpv_e = 2\,S_x\,/\,R_e$$

where *Re* = *empirical* Range

$$Cpv_s = 2\,S_x\,/\,R_s$$

where R_s = *scale* Range

The Coefficient of Proportional Variance, expressed in terms of the Formula of Maximum Variance of Messick

Messick (1982, p. 750) demonstrated that the variance of a *distribution of maximum variance* could be calculated using the following equation:

$$S^2{}_m = (X_b - X_a)^2 / 4$$

Where X_b is the *maximum score* and X_a is the *minimum score*. Therefore, we could express the *proportional relationship* between the *observed variance* $(S^2{}_x)$ and the *expected variance* $(S^2{}_\mathring{a})$ of a *distribution of maximum variance* in these terms:

$$[S^2{}_x / S^2{}_\mathring{a}] = S^2{}_x / [(X_b - X_a)^2 / 4]$$

$$[S^2{}_x / S^2{}_\mathring{a}] = S^2{}_x / (R^2{}_x / 4)$$

and therefore,

$$[S_x / S_\mathring{a}] = S_x / (R_x / 2)$$

$$[S_x / S_\mathring{a}] = 2 S_x / R_x$$

which is equal to the **Cpve**:

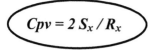

$$Cpv = 2\, S_x\, /\, R_x$$

CHAPTER 3

A COMPARATIVE ANALYSIS OF THE NEW

COEFFICIENT, USING DIFFERENT

PROTOTYPES OF DISTRIBUTIONS

Knowing the *Coefficient of Proportional*
Variance (*empirical* or *scalar*) of one   or more
distributions, any one can evaluate and compare in a
more appropriate form the corresponding relative
variances. By means of five examples, the concepts
involved will be clarified,   the different prototypes
of distributions to which the coefficient will be
applied will be clearly specified   (there   are   no

restrictions as for symmetry and kurtosis), and the fundamental properties of the new coefficient will be discussed when comparing it with the other conventional coefficients.

Example 1:

Comparing and evaluating the proportional variance in distributions with the same empirical range, each one expressed on the same scale base and measuring units.

Table 2 (Figures 4a to 4e) presents five distributions with the same empirical range: *Ai* is an equidistant uniform distribution (distance = 10), *Bi*

Table 2
Five Prototypes of Distributions (Ai, Bi, Ci, Di, Ei) with Equal Empirical Ranks (50-10=40), to Compare the Standard Deviations and the Two Versions of the Coefficient of Proportional Variance. Fictitious Data

Ai	f(Ai)	Bi	f(Bi)	Ci	f(Ci)	Di	f(Di)	Ei	f(Ei)
10	2	10	2	10	2	10	6	10	1
20	2	22	2	20	4	20	5	20	3
30	2	37	2	30	6	30	4	30	4
40	2	41	2	40	4	40	3	40	5
50	2	50	2	50	2	50	2	50	6

$M_A =$	$M_B =$	$M_C =$	$M_D =$	$M_E =$
30	32.0	30.0	25.0	36.3
$S_A =$	$S_B =$	$S_C =$	$S_D =$	$S_E =$
14.91(3)[1]	15.01(2)	11.88(5)	13.57(4)	17.06(1)
$N_A = 10$	$N_B = 10$	$N_C = 18$	$N_D = 20$	$N_E = 19$
$Cpv_{eA} =$	$Cpv_{eB} =$	$Cpv_{eC} =$	$Cpv_{eD} =$	$Cpv_{eE} =$
74.65(3)[2]	75.05(2)	59.40(5)	67.85(4)	88.25(1)
$Cpv_{sA} =$	$Cpv_{sB} =$	$Cpv_{sC} =$	$Cpv_{sD} =$	$Cpv_{sE} =$
69.44(3)	69.81(2)	55.26(5)	63.12(4)	82.09(1)
$R_{eA}^{3} = 40$	$R_{eB} = 40$	$R_{eC} = 40$	$R_{eD} = 40$	$R_{eE} = 40$
$R_{sA}^{3} = 43$	$R_{sB} = 43$	$R_{sC} = 43$	$R_{sD} = 43$	$R_{sE} = 43$

( )[1] = Rank order of the distribution, according to the corresponding Standard Deviations $(S_a, S_b, S_c, S_d, S_e)$.
( )[2] = Rank order of the distribution, according to Cpv_e (empirical Cpv) **and** Cpv_s (scale Cpv).
( )[3] = R_e (empirical range); R_s (scale range).

Note: The values of Cpv_e de Cpv_s are given in percentages.

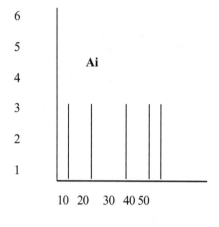

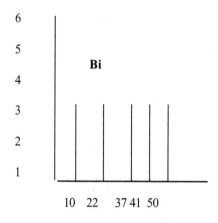

Figures 4a y 4b:
Two Prototypes of Distributions (Ai, Bi) with
Equal Empirical Ranges and Different
Variances. Data from Table 2

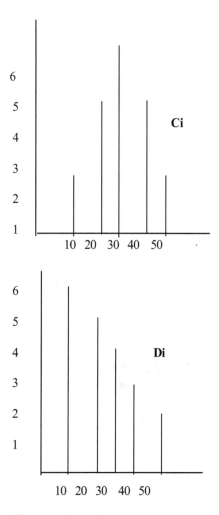

Figures 4c y 4d:
Two Prototypes of Distributions (Ci, Di) with
Equal Empirical Ranges and Different
Variances. Data from Table 2

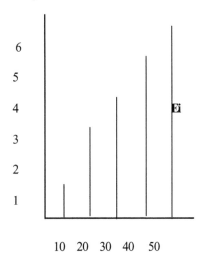

Figure 4e:
Prototype (Ei) of Equal Empirical Range
Distributions with Different Variances. Data from
Table 2

is a uniform distribution (distance = 10), *Ci* is a triangular distribution (N is even), *Di* is a distribution positively skewed and *Ei* is a distribution negatively skewed. Besides the mean and of the size of the sample, for each distribution the Cpv_e and the Cpv_s have been calculated. A ranking order was also assigned to each one of the coefficients values, according to its size (1 representing the highest range).

In the case of distributions with the same *empirical range*, the results clearly indicate a complete agreement between both ranges of the Cpv_e and Cpv_s, as well as with the corresponding standard deviations; however, the Cpv_e and the Cpv_s offer certain additional information, that of establishing the *proportional magnitude of the variability* within and across different distributions.

For example, in the Ai distribution the unbiased standard deviation is 14.91, but this value in itself does not offer complete information on "how big" or "how small" is the variability, independently of any of the other distributions. By means of the calculation of Cpv_e (74.65%) or of the Cpv_s (69.44%), we can affirm clearly that the *relative variability* is high, in the first case, and moderately high, in the second case:

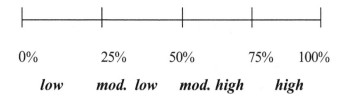

The differences of percentages between the Cpv_e and the Cpv_s are produced by the differences between R_e and R_s. It is expected that the differences of percentages should be directly proportional to the size of the difference between R_e and R_s ; therefore, the corresponding ranges should stay same.

When $R_e = R_s$, then $Cpv_e = Cpv_s$

Example 2:

Comparing and evaluating the Proportional Variance of distributions with unequal empirical ranges and equal scale ranges, each one expressed on the same measuring scale base and on the same measuring unit.

Table 3 (Figures 5a to 5e) contains five distributions which are unequal in their empirical ranges: *Ai* is an equidistant uniform distribution (the distance among the scores = 8), Bi is a non uniform non equidistant distribution, Ci is a triangular distribution, Di is a positively asymmetric distribution and Ei it is a negatively asymmetric distribution.

In this case, the ranges of the *Coefficient of Scale Proportional Variance (Cpv$_S$)* are in agreement with the corresponding standard deviations. However, the ranges of the ***Coefficient of Empirical Proportional Variance (Cpv$_e$)*** are not in agreement with the standard deviations. This could be explained by the fact that the ***Cpv$_s$*** is estimated using the same scale range (Rs = 40), making the quotients to have the same denominator; in other words, the ***Cpv$_s$*** represents a point within the *sampling space* of the *maximum variation* of the total number of scores or *expected observations* (*"expected sampling space"*). For this reason, it is more appropriate, when comparing different distributions, that those distributions be based on the same measuring scale. On the other hand, the ***Cpv$_e$*** uses a different denominator for each

Table 3

Five Prototypes of Distributions (Ai, Bi, Ci, Di, Ei) with Unequal Empirical Ranges and Equal Scale Ranges, to Compare the Corresponding Standard Deviations and the Two Versions of the Coefficient of Proportional Variance. Fictitious Data

Ai	F(Ai)	Bi	f(Bi)	Ci	f(Ci)	Di	f(Di)	Ei	f(Ei)
13	3	12	2	10	2	11	6	12	2
16	3	18	2	12	4	14	5	13	3
29	3	27	2	15	6	15	4	14	4
37	3	36	2	20	4	18	3	16	5
45	3	41	2	25	2	19	2	18	6
$M_A =$ 29.0		$M_B = 26.8$		$M_C =$ 16.00		$M_D = 11.9$		$M_E =$ 15.39	
$S_A =$ 11.17(2)[1]		$S_B =$ 11.38 (1)		$S_C =$ 4.65(3)		$S_D =$ 2.83(4)		$S_E = 2.19$ (5)	
$N_A = 15$		$N_B = 10$		$N_C = 18$		$N_D = 20$		$N_E = 20$	
$Cpv_{eA} =$ 69.81(2)[2]		$Cpv_{eB} =$ 78.48(1)		$Cpv_{eC} =$ 62.00(5)		$Cpv_{eD} =$ 70.75(4)		$Cpv_{eE} =$ 73.00(3)	
$Cpv_{sA} =$ 55.85(2)[2]		$Cpv_{sB} =$ 56.90(1)		$Cpv_{sC} =$ 23.25(3)		$Cpv_{sD} =$ 14.15(4)		$Cpv_{sE} =$ 10.95(5)	
$R_{sA}{}^3 = 45$- 05 = 40		$R_{sB} =$ 45-05 = 40		$R_{sC} =$ 45-05 = 40		$R_{sD} =$ 45-05 = 40		$R_{sE} =$ 45-05 = 40	
$R_{eA}{}^3 =$ 45-3=32		$R_{eB} =$ 4112=29		$R_{eC} =$ 2510=15		$R_{eD} = 19$- 11=8		$R_{eE} =$ 18–12=6	

( )[1] = Rank order of the distribution, according to the corresponding Standard Deviations $(S_a, S_b, S_c, S_d, S_e)$.
( )[2] = Rank order of the distribution, according to Cpv_e *(empirical Cpv)* **and** Cpv_s *(scale Cpv)*.
( )[3] = R_e *(empirical range);* R_s *(scale range).*

Note: The values of Cpv_e de Cpv_s are given in

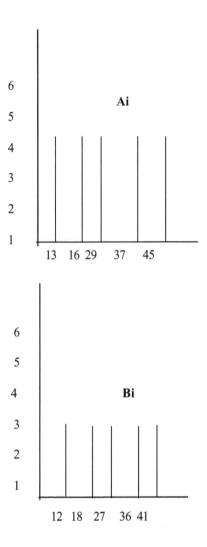

Figures 5a y 5b:
Two Prototypes (Ai, Bi) of Distributions with
Unequal Empirical Ranges. Data from Table 3.

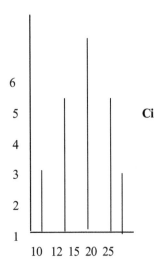

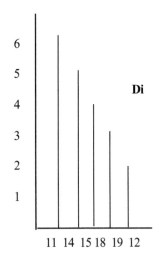

Figures 5c y 5c:
Two Prototypes (Ci, Di) of Distributions with
Unequal Empirical Ranges. Data from Table 3

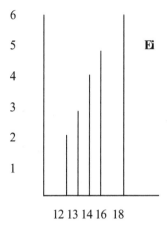

Figures 5e:
Prototype (Ei) of Distributions with
Unequal Empirical Ranges. Data from
Table 3

one of the quotients of the distributions, since R_{oa}

R_{ob} R_{oc}... R_{oz}; that is to say, each $\boldsymbol{Cpv_e}$ represents

a random point within   the *sample space* of the

maximum variation of the scores or observations

obtained empirically (*"empirical sampling space"*)

for each distribution. The $\boldsymbol{Cpv_e}$ constitutes a much

more significant measure of the $\boldsymbol{proportional}$

$\boldsymbol{variance}$ within each distribution, independently of

the other distributions. This is particularly certain

when we are only interested in the variability $\boldsymbol{within}$

the total group of observed or empirical scores of a

given distribution.

For example, according to Table 3, the

distribution with the highest variability $\boldsymbol{within}$ is *Bi,*

$Cpv_e = 78.48$, and the one that has higher variability

between is also *Bi, Cpv_s = 56.90,* both having a range of 1. For the distributions *Ci, Di and Di,* the ranges do not coincide. The ***Cpv_e*** allows for *a much more relevant interpretation on the magnitude of the variability* ***within*** *each distribution, while the* ***Cpv_s*** *allows for a better comparison* ***among*** *or* ***between*** *different distributions.*

Example 3:

Comparing and evaluating the proportional variances of two distributions with different but equivalent scale bases

In Table 4 two distributions appear with different but equivalent scale bases (Ai, weight in kilograms and Bi, weight in pounds). The first one is an *uniform non-equidistant distribution* (distances

D1 = 20, D2 = 5, among the values of the variable) and the other one is *also a uniform non-equidistant distribution* (D1 = 24.6, D2 = 6.0). When the standard deviations are observed, the variability of *Ai* is more or less equivalent to the variability of *Bi*. Again, the rank orderings of *Sa, Sb, and Cpvs$_s$* coincide, but a more precise information is obtained when the *Cpv$_s$* is used instead of only Sa or Sb. ***Within*** each distribution, *Bi (90.24%)* appears with a relative variability very similar to that of *Ai (Cpv$_e$ = 90.27%)*.

Table 4
Comparing and Evaluating the Proportional Variance of Two
Distributions Ai, Bi) with Different but Equivalent Scale Bases.
*Unequal **Empirical Ranges**. Equal Scale Ranges.* **Ratio Measuring**
Scale. Fictitious Data.

Ai	f(Ai)	Bi	f(Bi)
68	4	81.6	4
48	4	57.6	4
43	4	51.6	4
Ai = peso en Kgs.		*Bi = weight in Pounds.*	
$M_A = 53.00;$		$M_B = 63.60;$	
$M_{nA} = 48;$		$M_{nA} = 57.60;$	
$P_{25} = 43;$		$P_{25} = 51,60;$	
$P_{75} = 68$		$P_{75} = 81,60$	
$S_A = 11.2815(1)^1$		$S_B = 13.5378(2)$	
$N_A = 12$		$N_B = 12$	
$Cpv_{eA} =$		$Cpv_{eB} =$	
90.24 [1]^2		90.27 [1]	
$Cpv_{sA} =$		$Cpv_{sB} =$	
22.56 [1]^2		27.08 [2]	
$R_{eA} = 25 (1)^3$		$R_{eB} = 30 (2)$	
$R_{sA} = (100-00) =$		$R_{sB} = (100-00) =$	
$100 (1)^4$		$100 (1)$	
$Q_{1A} = 43;$		$Q_{1B} = 51.60;$	
$Q_{3A} = 68$		$Q_{3B} = 81.60$	

( )^1 = Rank order of the distribution, according to the
    corresponding Standard Deviations *(S$_A$, S$_B$)*.
[ ]^2 = Rank order of the distribution, according to *Cpv$_e$*
    *(empirical Cpv) **and** Cpv$_s$ (scale Cpv)*.
( )^3 = Rank order of the distribution , according to *R$_e$*
    (Empirical Range).
( )^4 = Rank order of the distribution , according to *R$_s$*
    (Scale Range).
Bi = 1.20 **Ai*; Kgs = 1.20 * Lbs.; *M* (Arithmetic Mean);
    M$_n$ (Median); *Q$_1$* (Quartile1); *Q$_3$* (Quartile 3)

Note: The values of *Cpv$_e$* de *Cpv$_s$* are given in

Example 4: Comparing and evaluating two or more distributions, each one expressed in different and non-equivalent scales bases

Two distributions with *different and non-equivalent scale bases* (height measured in centimeters and weight measured in kilograms) are presented in Table 5. Since the two scales are not equivalent (the linear transformation of centimeters to kilograms does not exist), the only possibility to calculate the Cpv_s and the Cpv_e is by arbitrarily establishing the maximum and minimum value of each distribution. It is interesting to observe that the ranges of the corresponding standard deviations, of the Cpv_e and of the Cpv_s coefficients, all coincide. However, taking into consideration only the

Table 5
Comparing and Evaluating the Proportional Variance of Two Distributions (Ci, Di) with Different and Non Equivalent Scale Bases. Ratio Measuring Scale. Fictitious Data.

Ci	f(Ci)	Di	f(Di)
165	3	52	10
174	4	72	5
176	5	78	7
181	2	79	9

Ci = **height in cms.**   *Di* = **weight in kgs.**

$M_C = 173.79; Mn_C = 175.00;$ $M_D = 68.94; Mn_D = 78.00;$

$P_{25} = 171,75; P_{75} = 176$ $P_{25} = 52; P_{75} = 79$

$S_C = 5.2750 \ (2)^1$ $S_D = 12.1132 \ (1)$

$N_C = 14$ $N_D = 31$

$Cpv_{eC} = 66.00 \ [2]^2$ $Cpv_{eD} = 89.70 \ [1]$

$Cpv_{sC} = 21.12 \ [2]$ $Cpv_{sD} = 48.44 \ [1]$

$R_{eC} = 16 \ (1)^3$ $R_{eD} = 27 \ (2)$

$R_{sC} = 200 - 150 = 50 \ (1)^4$ $R_{sD} = 100 - 50 = 50 \ (1)$

( )[1] = Rank order of the distribution, according to the corresponding Standard Deviations *(S_C,, S_D)*.
[ ][2] = Rank order of the distribution, according to *Cpv_e (empirical Cpv) and Cpv_s (scale Cpv)*.
( )[3] = Rank order of the distribution , according to *R_e (Empirical Range)*.
( )[4] = Rank order of the distribution , according to *R_s (Scale Range)*.

Re (Empirical Range), Rs (Scale Range), M (Arithmetic Mean); M_n(Median), P_25 , P_75 (Percentile 25, Percentile 75)

Note: The values of *Cpv_e* de *Cpv_s* are given in percentages.

standard deviations, the variability of the distribution Di is a little more than twice as big as the one of the distribution Ci, while the same difference is only of .03% (90.27 - 90.24) among the ***Cpv*$_e$** coefficients *and of 4.52% (27.08 - 22.56) among the values of the **Cpv*$_s$** coefficients. These differences can be explained by virtue of the existent proportional relationship between the Standard Deviation and the Range (empirical and scalar), in each one of those distributions.

In Table 5, the corresponding *medians* were estimated, for the purpose of facilitating the interpretation of the observed variability, given that the two distributions are asymmetric (especially distribution Di).

Knowing that the Standard Deviation is the average distance between each one of the scores and the arithmetic mean, it is clear that in the case of asymmetric distributions (such as Di) the variability measured by Sx is not the most appropriate approach. Also, in this example the two distributions are not equivalent in relation to their scale base, and therefore the corresponding standard deviations do not allow for a comparison of variability *between* the two distributions.

Comparison between the Conventional Coefficients of Relative Variability and the Coefficient of Proportional Variance. Sensibility: Stability and Consistency

The ***property of stability*** is defined here as the metric property of a given coefficient of staying relatively stable or constant when the distribution has been transformed in such way that the values of the variable change, but without affecting the relative variability (adding, or multiplying for a constant, for example).

The ***property of consistency*** is defined as *the metric property of a given coefficient of changing in its magnitude when the distribution has been transformed in such way that the values of the variable change, affecting the relative variability* (altering the minimum and maximum values, for example).

To determine the **stability** and the **consistency** of the **Cpv** when it is compared with the conventional coefficients, two groups of distributions have been used: the first one consisting of two distributions with *different but equivalent scale bases* (distributions **Ai** and **Bi,** Table 4) .The second group is made up of two distributions with *different and non equivalent scale bases* (distributions **Ci** and **Di**, Table 5). The coefficients of *relative variability* calculated initially are presented in Table 6 . The corresponding values obtained as the products of the *transformations* carried out *(Transformation T1 = 20 + Xi; Transformation T2 = 20 * Xi and Transformation T3 = substitution of one or two of the minimum or* *maximum scores for arbitrary values, generating changes in the relative variability)*, are presented in Tables 7, 8 and 9 (Figures 6 to 12). Figure 13 presents the values of the ratio between the Standard Deviation and the Empirical Range ($Q = S_x / R_e$).

According to Table 6, the values of Cpv_e are the highest in the four distributions, while the values of the CMD are the lowest. The values of the obtained Cpv_s of the CMD are the lowest. The values of the obtained Cpv_s are always smaller than those of the Cpv_e; only when the *Empirical Range (R$_e$)* and the *Scale Range (R$_s$)* are the same, the Cpv_e and Cpv_s would be the same *(in general, the range of the empirical values is smaller)*. The values of the

Cpv_e, as demonstrated before, represent the *true proportional relationship between the observed variability and the expected maximum variability.* The coefficients CV and CQV are the same in the first two distributions, and they tend to be similar in the last two. The other coefficients are completely different. The values of the Cpv_e are directly proportional to the relationship of the ratio $Q = Sx/Re.$

According to Tables 7 and 8, the Cpv in its two forms of Cpv_e and Cpv_s, demonstrates a complete stability (these two forms do not change

Table 6
Comparison of the Different Coefficients of Relative Variance, in Relation to Four Prototypes of Distributions (Ai, Bi, Ci y Di).

Dist	CV	CR	CMD	CDMDM	CQV
Ai	.2129	.4505	.1887	.1736	.4505
Bi	.2129	.4505	.1887	.1572	.4505
Ci	.0304	.0925	.0217	.0302	.0244
Di	.1757	.4122	.1585	.1237	.4122

Dist	Cpv_e	Cpv_s	S_x	R_e	R_s	Q
Ai	.9024	.2256	11.28	25.0	100	.4512
Bi	.9027	.2708	13.54	30.0	100	.4513
Ci	.6600	.2112	05.28	16.0	50	.3300
Di	.8970	.4844	12.11	27.0	50	.4485

Note: The values of the relative variability coefficients
are expressed in proportions

CV = Coefficient of Variance; CR = Coefficient of Range; CMD = Coefficient of Mean Deviation; $CMDND$ = Coefficient of Median Deviation; CQV = Coefficient of Quartile Variation; Cpv_e = Coefficient of Empirical Proportional Variance; Cpv_s = Coefficient of Scale Proportional Variance ; S_x = Standard Deviation; R_e = Empirical Range; R_s = Scale Range; $Q = S_x / R_s$.

Table 7
Analysis of Sensibility of the Different Coefficients
Of Relative Variability. Criterion of Stability
Transformation T1 : Yi = Xi + 20.

Dist	CV	CR	CMD	CMDND	CQV
Ai	.1545	.3311	.2740	.2206	.3311
Bi	.0198	.3464	.0221	.1735	.3464
Ci	.0272	.0829	.5201	.5425	.0219
Di	.1362	.3158	.1103	.1149	.3158

Dist	Cpv_e	Cpv_s	S_x	R_e	R_s	Q
Ai	.9024	.2256	11.28	25.0	100	.4512
Bi	.9027	.2708	13.54	30.0	100	.4513
Ci	.6600	.2112	05.28	16.0	50	.3300
Di	.8970	.4844	12.11	27.0	50	.4485

Note: The values of the relative variability coefficients
are expressed in proportions

CV = Coefficient of Variance; CR = Coefficient of Range; CMD = Coefficient of Mean Deviation; $CMDND$ = Coefficient of Median Deviation; CQV = Coefficient of Quartile Variation; Cpv_e = Coefficient of Empirical Proportional Variance; Cpv_s = Coefficient of Scale Proportional Variance ; S_x = Standard Deviation; R_e = Empirical Range; R_s = Scale Range; $Q = S_x / R_s$.

Table 8
Analysis of Sensibility of the Different Coefficients
Of Relative Variability. Criterion of Stability
Transformation T1 : Yi = 20 Xi.

Dist	CV	CR	CMD	CMDND	CQV
Ai	.2129	.4505	.9500	.9498	.4505
Bi	.2129	.4505	.7833	.7781	.4505
Ci	.0303	.0925	.2550	.2246	.0244
Di	.1757	.4122	.7188	.5712	.4122

Dist	Cpv_e	Cpv_s	S_x	R_e	R_s	Q
Ai	.9024	.2256	225.63	500	100	.4512
Bi	.9027	.2708	270.76	600	100	.4513
Ci	.6600	.2106	105.30	320	50	.3300
Di	.8970	.4845	242.26	540	50	.4485

Note: The values of the relative variability coefficients
are expressed in proportions

CV = Coefficient of Variance; CR = Coefficient of Range; CMD = Coefficient of Mean Deviation; $CMDND$ = Coefficient of Median Deviation; CQV = Coefficient of Quartile Variation; Cpv_e = Coefficient of Empirical Proportional Variance; Cpv_s = Coefficient of Scale Proportional Variance ; S_x = Standard Deviation; R_e = Empirical Range; R_s = Scale Range; $Q = S_x / R_s$.

Table 9
Analysis of Sensibility of the Different Coefficients
Of Relative Variability. Criterion of Consistency
Transformation T3: Substitution of One or Two Scores
(Minimum and Maximum) by Arbitrary Values,
Generating Changes in Relative Variability

Dist	CV	CR	CMD	CMDND	CQV
Ai	.4023	1.358	.2257	.2257	.4505
Bi	.4774	1.759	.3276	.3178	.4505
Ci	.0890	.2911	.0619	.0453	.0244
Di	.1990	.6133	.1670	.1394	.4122

Dist	Cpv_e	Cpv_s	S_x	R_e	R_s	Q
Ai	.7022	.3862	19.31	55	100	.3511
Bi	.6984	.5334	26.67	76.4	100	.3492
Ci	.6557	.6032	15.08	46	50	.3278
Di	.6070	.5584	13.96	46	50	.3035

*Notice that in this transformation the values of **CR** are **greater** than unity in the distributions **Ai** y **Bi** (**CR** does not represent a true proportional variability)*

Note: The values of the relative variability coefficients are expressed in proportions

CV = Coefficient of Variance; CR = Coefficient of Range; CMD = Coefficient of Mean Deviation; $CMDND$ = Coefficient of Median Deviation; CQV = Coefficient of Quartile Variation; Cpv_e = Coefficient of Empirical Proportional Variance; Cpv_s = Coefficient of Scale Proportional Variance; S_x = Standard Deviation; R_e = Empirical Range; R_s = Scale Range; $Q = S_x / R_s$.

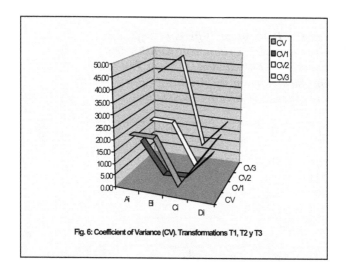

Fig. 6: Coefficient of Variance (CV). Transformations T1, T2 y T3

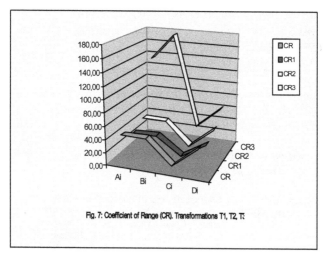

Fig. 7: Coefficient of Range (CR). Transformations T1, T2, T3

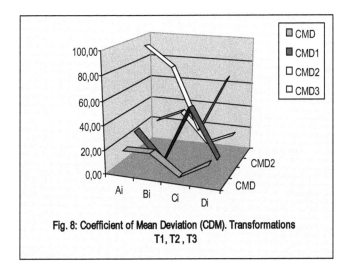

Fig. 8: Coefficient of Mean Deviation (CDM). Transformations T1, T2, T3

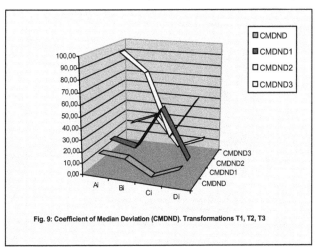

Fig. 9: Coefficient of Median Deviation (CMDND). Transformations T1, T2, T3

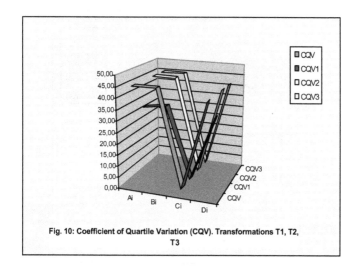

Fig. 10: Coefficient of Quartile Variation (CQV). Transformations T1, T2, T3

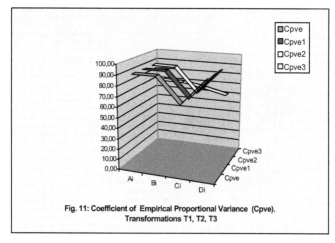

Fig. 11: Coefficient of Empirical Proportional Variance (Cpve). Transformations T1, T2, T3

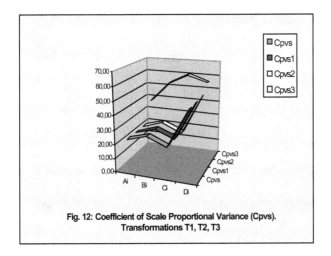

Fig. 12: Coefficient of Scale Proportional Variance (Cpvs). Transformations T1, T2, T3

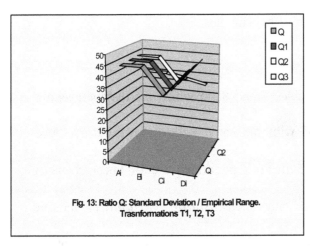

Fig. 13: Ratio Q: Standard Deviation / Empirical Range. Trasnformations T1, T2, T3

since the relative variability of the distributions stay the same). All the other coefficients show to be unstable, especially coefficient *CV*; for example, according to Table 7, in distribution *Bi* (from .2129 in Table 6, to .0198 in Table 7) and in the distribution *Di* (from .1757 in Table 6, to.1362 in Table 7). All the other coefficients vary considerably (they are unstable).

Tables 7 and 8 (in which the distributions are presented with the same *relative variability*, since the transformations performed are of lineal character modifying only the *absolute variability*) indicate clearly how the Cpv_e is modified as a function of the ratio or proportional relationship between the two measures of variability: the *standard deviation* and the *empirical range*. The obtained value of the Cpv_e is *directly proportional* to each one of the values of the ratio Sx/Re. Because of this, the highest value in the $Cpve$ (.9027) corresponds to the highest value of the quotient S_x/R_e (.4513), and the lowest value in the $Cpve$ (.6600) corresponds to the lowest quotient of S_x/R_e (.3300).

These changes observed in the Cpv_e are absolutely *consistent* with the changes in the *relative variability* (measured in terms of both the *standard deviation* and of the *empirical range*) of the corresponding transformed distributions.

The *conventional coefficients* also make certain adjustments for the corresponding changes in variability. However, *since these conventional coefficients are not based in a clear and demonstrated mathematical relationship among the terms upon which they are defined, they are both **unstable** and **inconsistent***.

These properties of **stability** and **consistency** of the *Cpv* are even more evident in Figures 6 to 12, in which the values for each of the coefficients of variability are represented as a function of the three data transformations: T1, T2 and T3. It should be noticed that *transformation T3 is the only one that produces changes in the relative variability* of the corresponding distributions, and therefore, *all the coefficients should be consistent and to change only in T3.* However, the coefficients *CV* (Figure 6), *CR* (Figure 7), *CMD* (Figure 8) and *CMDND* (Figure 9), vary considerably in transformations T1 and T2, demonstrating *instability*. The *CQV* (Figure 10) stays stable in transformation T2; however, it also stays stable (against expectation) in transformation T3, when in fact it should have changed. *The coefficient Cpv_e (Figure 11) and the coefficient Cpv_s (Figure 12) demonstrated stability and consistency, given that they stay constant after transformations T1 and T2.* Since there are changes in the *relative variability,* the values *change considerably in T3*. Figure 11 *(Cpv_e)* coincides exactly with Figure 13

(Q = Sx/Re), given that both coefficients measure the same *relative variability*, using different measuring scales.

CHAPTER 4

ADVANTAGES AND DISADVANTAGES OF

THE *COEFFICIENT OF PROPORTIONAL*

VARIANCE (Cpv)

Advantages:

1. - Easiness and speed when calculating it, once the standard deviation is known. In most cases, when research data is reported, usually the corresponding arithmetic means and standard deviations are included.

2. - The calculated value of the **Cpv** may be expressed in percentages by multiplying for the constant 100.

3. - Since $(0.00 \leq \textbf{Cpv} \leq 1.00)$, or $(0.0\% \leq \textbf{Cpv} \leq 100\%)$, it becomes easier the interpretation of the results using the following evaluation scale:

$(0.0 \leq \textbf{Cpv} \leq .25) = $ low

$(.26 \leq \textbf{Cpv} \leq .50) = $ moderately low

$(.51 \leq \textbf{Cpv} \leq .75) = $ moderately high

$(.76 \leq \textbf{Cpv} \leq 1.00) = $ high

4. - The **Cpv** indicates the *true proportional relationship* between the *observed specific variance*

(absolute) of the obtained data and the *attainable maximum variance* on the corresponding scale. In particular, the ***Cpv*** can be considered as an standardization procedure for the comparison of variability among distributions with different measuring scales and with major differences on the magnitude of their standard deviations.

5. - The *form of the distribution* (asymmetry and/or kurtosis) does not affect the calculation neither the meaning of the ***Cpv***.

6. - The ***Cpv*** can be used to compare and to evaluate two or more distributions simultaneously.

7. - The *Cpv* is particularly useful when two or more distributions are compared and the scores or observations have been obtained using different measuring scales or different units of measure.

8. - The *Cpv* has the fundamental property of being the most sensitive in the determination of the *relative variability* of a given distribution, in terms of *stability* and *consistency*, when it is compared to the *conventional coefficients*: *Coefficient of Variance (CV), Coefficient of Range (CR), Coefficient of Mean Deviation (CMD), Coefficient of Median Deviation (CMDND), Coefficient of Quartile Variance (CQV).*

9. - When using statistical packages such as the SPSS, the calculation of the Cpv_e and of the Cpv_s is even easier.

In the Appendixes of this book some programs in SPSS for the calculation of Cpv_s, Cpv_e and the different conventional coefficients have been included.

Disadvantages:

1. - By definition, it is not possible to calculate the Cpv_s or the Cpv_e, unless the standard deviation and either the *scale range* or the *empirical range*, are known.

2. - The *Cpv* should not be considered as a *substitute* of the standard deviation (which only measures *absolute variability*), but rather a complementary and different procedure to evaluate in a more appropriate form the *relative variability* of data.

3. - The *Cpv*, as the standard deviation, requires that the variable of the distribution be measured at least an *interval scale*. For distributions with nominal or ordinal scales, the *Cpv* is not computable.

4. - In general, the Cpv_e *is always higher than the Cpvs. In practice, the* Cpv_e *is the most*

commonly   used, since in many occasions the true

scale range is unknown. In this sense, the $\boldsymbol{Cpv_e}$ tends

to overestimate the true relative variability.

CHAPTER 5

CONCLUSIONS AND RECOMMENDATIONS

Summary

The fundamental problem of measuring and evaluating the *relative variation* of a given data distribution has been discussed by different authors and, in an intent to solve it, some *conventional coefficients* have already been developed: *Coefficient of Variance (CV), Coefficient of Range (CR), Coefficient of Mean Deviation (CMD), and the Coefficient of Quartile Variation (CQV).* When these coefficients are analyzed, it is observed that they lack an essential property: ***they do not define a clear***

mathematical relationship of the terms upon which they were developed. This generates some problems when interpreting the obtained values for each of the coefficients, as well as when trying to convert each other or to compare them.

In this paper, a new coefficient is proposed: the ***Coefficient of Proportional Variance (Cpv)***. Defined as the ratio between two times the Standard Deviation and the Range (Empirical or Scale Range). This new coefficient demonstrates a clear mathematical relationship between its defining components (Standard Deviation, Range and Maximum Variability), allowing for a better and more complete interpretation of the relative variation of a given data distribution. There are two versions or forms: the ***Coefficient of Scale Proportional Variance (Cpv$_s$)*** and the ***Coefficient of Empirical Proportional Variance (Cpv$_e$)***, when either the *Scale Range* or the *Empirical Range* is used as denominator of the equation. These coefficients constitute two simple standardization procedures of the *proportional variability* among two or more distributions, for the purposes of making descriptive comparisons ***within*** and ***between*** them on ***relative variability***.

REFERENCES

García Hoz, V. y Ferrer Martín, S. (1966) **Estadística aplicada a la educación y ciencias humanas. I Estadística descriptiva**. Madrid, España: Ediciones Rialp, S.A.

Garret, H. E. (1926). **Statistics in psychology and education**. New York: Longmans, Green and Co.

Garret, H. E. (1976). **Estadística en psicología y educación.** (Trad. J. J. Thomas). Buenos Aires, Argentina: Editorial Piados. (Original en Inglés, 1947).

Hays, W. L. (1973). **Statistics for the social sciences**. (Second edition). New York: Holt, Rinehart and Winston, Inc.

Hernández-Nieto, R. A. (1980). **El desarrollo de un nuevo coeficiente para evaluar descriptivamente la variación relativa de un conjunto de datos.** Trabajo presentado en la XXX Convención Nacional de ASOVAC (Asociación Venezolana para el Avance de la Ciencia); Mérida, Venezuela: 9 al 14 de Noviembre.

Hernández-Nieto, R. A. (2000a). **Biostatistical implications of a comparative analysis on the *stability* and *consistency* of some** conventional relative variability coefficients and the *Coefficient of Proportional Variance (Cpv)*. Davis, California (USA): *SILCIBIO (Symposium of Latin-American Scientists in Biomedical Sciences)*, University of California – Davis, September 17 – 21.

Hernández-Nieto, R. A. (2000b). **Análisis comparativo de la sensibilidad (estabilidad y consistencia) de varios coeficientes de variación relativa y el Coeficiente de Variación Proporcional (Cvp) en diferentes prototipos de distribuciones aleatorias.** Trabajo presentado en la *L CONVENCIÓN NACIONAL DE ASOVAC* (Asociación Venezolana para el Avance de la Ciencia). Caracas, Venezuela (Universidad "Simón Bolívar"), 19 al 24 de Noviembre.

Hernández Nieto, R. A. (2001). **Contribuciones al análisis estadístico.** Mérida, Venezuela: Coedición de la Universidad de Los Andes (Facultad de Ciencias Jurídicas, Políticas y Criminológicas) y IESINFO (Instituto de Estudios en Informática). Available thru Greatunpublished.com booksurge.com and Amazon.com

Marascuilo, L. A. and Serlin, R. C. (1988). **Statistical methods for the social and behavioral sciences**. New York: W. H. Freeman and Company.

Messick, D. M. (1982). Some cheap tricks for making inferences about distribution shapes from variances. **Educational and Psychological Measurement, 42,** 749- 758.

Mosteller, F. and Rourke, R. E. (1973). **Sturdy statistics. Nonparametric and order statistics.** Reading, Massachussets: Addison-Wesley

Shao, S. P. (1972). **Estadística para economistas y administradores de empresas.** (Trad. R.E. Madrigal). México: Herrero Hermanos, Sucs., S.A. 1972 (Original en Inglés, 1967).

SPSS (1999). **SPSS Base 9.0. Applications guide.** Chicago, Illinois: Spss Inc.

APPENDIXES

DATA FILE OF FOUR PROTOTYPES OF DISTRIBUTIONS

Ai	Bi	Ci	Di
68,00	81,60	165,00	52,00
68,00	81,60	165,00	52,00
68,00	81,60	165,00	52,00
68,00	81,60	174,00	52,00
48,00	57,60	174,00	52,00
48,00	57,60	174,00	52,00
48,00	57,60	174,00	52,00
48,00	57,60	176,00	52,00
43,00	51,60	176,00	52,00
43,00	51,60	176,00	52,00
43,00	51,60	176,00	72,00
43,00	51,60	176,00	72,00
		181,00	72,00
		181,00	72,00
			72,00
			78,00
			78,00
			78,00
			78,00
			78,00
			78,00
			79,00
			79,00
			79,00
			79,00
			79,00
			79,00
			79,00
			79,00
			79,00

PROGRAMS IN SPSS TO CALCULATE THE
COEFFICIENTS OF RELATIVE VARIABILITY

----

* MEASURES OF CENTRAL TENDENCY, VARIABILITY,
EMPÍRICAL RANGE,
* P25, P75, MAXIMUM, MINIMUM:

FREQUENCIES
 VARIABLES=ai bi ci di
 /PERCENTILES= 25 75
 /STATISTICS=STDDEV RANGE MINIMUM MAXIMUM
MEAN MEDIAN MODE
 /ORDER ANALYSIS .

CALCULATION OF THE SUM OF ABSOLUTE
DESVIATIONS FROM THE MEAN AND THE MEDIAN:

RECODE
 num
 (1 thru 12=1) (13 thru 24=2) (25 thru 38=3) (39 thru
69=4) INTO
 distrib .
EXECUTE .

USE ALL.
COMPUTE filter_$=(distrib = 1).
VARIABLE LABEL filter_$ 'distrib = 1 (FILTER)'.
VALUE LABELS filter_$ 0 'Not Selected' 1 'Selected'.
FORMAT filter_$ (f1.0).
FILTER BY filter_$.
EXECUTE .

COMPUTE STANDEV1 = 11.28.
COMPUTE MEAN = 53.
COMPUTE MEDIAN = 48.
COMPUTE DIFM1 = (valor - MEDIA).

```
COMPUTE DIFMD1 = valor - MEDIAN).
COMPUTE devm1 = ABS (DIFM1).
COMPUTE devmD1 = ABS (DIFMD1).

FREQUENCIES
 VARIABLES=devm1 devmD1
 /STATISTICS=SUM
 /ORDER  ANALYSIS .

USE ALL.
COMPUTE filter_$=(distrib = 2).
VARIABLE LABEL filter_$ 'distrib = 2 (FILTER)'.
VALUE LABELS filter_$ 0 'Not Selected' 1 'Selected'.
FORMAT filter_$ (f1.0).
FILTER BY filter_$.
EXECUTE .

COMPUTE STANDEV2 = 13.54.
COMPUTE MEAN = 63.60.
COMPUTE MEDIAN =57.60.
COMPUTE DIFM2 = (valor - MEAN).
COMPUTE DIFMD2 = (valor - MEDIAN).
COMPUTE devm2 = ABS (DIFM2).
COMPUTE devmD2 = ABS (DIFMD2).

FREQUENCIES
 VARIABLES=devm2 devmD2
 /STATISTICS=SUM
 /ORDER  ANALYSIS .

USE ALL.
COMPUTE filter_$=(distrib = 3).
VARIABLE LABEL filter_$ 'distrib = 3 (FILTER)'.
VALUE LABELS filter_$ 0 'Not Selected' 1 'Selected'.
FORMAT filter_$ (f1.0).
FILTER BY filter_$.
EXECUTE .

COMPUTE STANDEV3 = 5.28.
```

```
COMPUTE MEAN =173.79.
COMPUTE MEDIAN =175.
COMPUTE DIFM3 = (valor - MEAN).
COMPUTE DIFMD3 = (valor - MEDIAN).
COMPUTE devm3 = ABS (DIFM3).
COMPUTE devmD3 = ABS (DIFMD3).

FREQUENCIES
 VARIABLES=devm3 devmD3
 /STATISTICS=SUM
 /ORDER  ANALYSIS .

USE ALL.
COMPUTE filter_$=(distrib = 4).
VARIABLE LABEL filter_$ 'distrib = 4 (FILTER)'.
VALUE LABELS filter_$  0 'Not Selected' 1 'Selected'.
FORMAT filter_$ (f1.0).
FILTER BY filter_$.
EXECUTE .

COMPUTE STANDEV4 = 12.11.
COMPUTE MEAN = 68.94.
COMPUTE MEDIAN = 78.
COMPUTE DIFM4 = (valor - MEAN) .
COMPUTE DIFMD4 = (valor - MEDIAN).
COMPUTE devm4 = ABS (DIFM4).
COMPUTE devmD4 = ABS (DIFMD4).

FREQUENCIES
 VARIABLES=devm4 devmD4
 /STATISTICS=SUM
 ORDER  ANALYSIS ./
```

PROGRAMS IN SPSS TO CALCULATE THE COEFFICIENTS OF RELATIVE VARIABILITY

```
COMPUTE CV = (STANDEV / MEAN)  * 100.
VARIABLE LABELS CV 'Coef. of Variance' .
EXECUTE .
COMPUTE CR = (RANGE_e /((minimum + maximum) / 2)) *
100.
VARIABLE LABELS CR 'Coef. Of Range' .
EXECUTE .
COMPUTE CMD = ((sumdmed / n)  / MEAN) * 100 .
VARIABLE LABELS CMD 'Coef. Of Mean Dev'.
EXECUTE.
COMPUTE CMDND = ((sumdmdn / n)  / MEDIAN) * 100.
VARIABLE LABELS CMDND 'Coef. Median Deviation' .
EXECUTE .
COMPUTE CQV = ((p75 - p25) / ((p25 + p75)/ 2)) * 100 .
VARIABLE LABELS CQV 'Coef. Quartile Variance' .
EXECUTE .
COMPUTE CpvE = ((2 * STANDEV) / RANGE_e) * 100 .
VARIABLE LABELS CpvE 'Coef. Emp. Prop. Var.' .
EXECUTE .
COMPUTE CpvS = ((2 * STANDEV) / RANGE_s) * 100 .
VARIABLE LABELS CpvS 'Coef. Scale Prop. Var.' .
EXECUTE .
COMPUTE Q = STANDEV / RANGE_e .
VARIABLE LABELS Q 'Ratio St. Dev - Re' .
EXECUTE .

LIST  VARIABLES=dist cv cr CQV cvpe cvps STANDEV
LIST  VARIABLES=dist CMD CMDND RANGE_e RANGE_s  Q.
```

PROGRAM IN SPSS. TRANSFORMATIONS T1,T2

```
--------------------------------------------------------
COMPUTE transf11 = ai + 20 . EXECUTE .
COMPUTE transf12 = bi + 20 . EXECUTE .
COMPUTE transf13 = ci + 20 . EXECUTE .
COMPUTE transf14 = di + 20 . EXECUTE .
COMPUTE transf21 = 20 * ai . EXECUTE .
COMPUTE transf22 = 20 * bi . EXECUTE .
COMPUTE transf23 = 20 * ci . EXECUTE .
COMPUTE transf24 = 20 * di . EXECUTE .


FREQUENCIES
  VARIABLES=transf11 transf12 transf13
transf14 transf21 transf22 transf23
  transf24 /PERCENTILES= 25 75
/STATISTICS=STDDEV RANGE MINIMUM MAXIMUM
MEAN
  MEDIAN /ORDER  ANALYSIS .
```

OUTPUT OF THE SPSS PROGRAMS TO CALCULATE THE COEFFICIENTS OF RELATIVE VARIABILITY

Original Distributions: No Transformation

DIST	CV	CR	CMD	CMDND	CQV	CPVE	CPVS
Ai	21.28	45.05	18.87	17.36	45.05	90.24	22.56
Bi	21.29	45.05	18.87	15.72	45.05	90.27	27.08
Ci	3.04	9.25	2.17	3.02	2.44	66.00	21.12
Di	17.57	41.22	15.85	12.37	41.22	89.70	48.44

Number of cases read: 4   Number of cases listed: 4

DIST	STANDEV	RANGE_E	RANGE_S	Q
Ai	11.28	25.00	100.00	.4512
Bi	13.54	30.00	100.00	.4513
Ci	5.28	16.00	50.00	.3300
Di	12.11	27.00	50.00	.4485

Number of cases read: 4   Number of cases listed: 4

Transformation $T1 = 20 + Xi$

DIST	CV	CR	CMD	CMDND	CQV	CPVE	CPVS
Ai	15.45	33.11	27.40	22.06	33.11	90.24	22.56
Bi	1.98	34.64	2.21	17.35	34.64	90.27	27.08
Ci	2.72	8.29	52.01	54.25	2.19	66.00	21.12
Di	13.62	31.58	11.03	11.49	31.58	89.70	48.44

Number of cases read: 4   Number of cases listed: 4

DIST	STANDEV	RANGE_E	RANGE_S	Q
Ai	11.28	25.00	100.00	.4512
Bi	13.54	30.00	100.00	.4513
Ci	5.28	16.00	50.00	.3300
Di	12.11	27.00	50.00	.4485

Number of cases read: 4   Number of cases listed: 4

Transformation T2: 20*Xi

DIST	CV	CR	CMD	CMDND	CQV	CPVE	CPVS
Ai	21.29	45.05	95.00	94.48	45.05	90.25	22.56
Bi	21.29	45.05	78.33	77.81	45.05	90.25	27.08
Ci	3.03	9.25	25.50	22.46	2.44	65.81	21.06
Di	17.57	41.22	71.88	57.12	41.22	89.73	48.45

Number of cases read: 4   Number of cases listed: 4

DIST	STANDEV	RANGE_E	RANGE_S	Q
Ai	225.63	500.00	2000.00	.4513
Bi	270.76	600.00	2000.00	.4513
Ci	105.30	320.00	1000.00	.3291
Di	242.26	540.00	1000.00	.4486

Number of cases read: 4   Number of cases listed: 4

Transformation T3: Substitution of One or Two Arbitrary Values

DIST	CV	CR	CMD	CMDND	CQV	CPVE	CPVS
Ai	40.23	135.80	22.57	22.57	45.05	70.22	38.62
Bi	47.74	175.91	32.76	31.78	45.05	69.84	53.34
Ci	8.90	29.11	6.19	4.53	2.44	65.57	60.32
Di	19.90	61.33	16.70	13.94	41.22	60.70	55.84

Number of cases read: 4   Number of cases listed: 4

DIST   STANDEV RANGE_E RANGE_S Q

Ai	19.31	55.00	100.00	.3511
Bi	26.67	76.37	100.00	.3492
Ci	15.08	46.00	50.00	.3278
Di	13.96	46.00	50.00	.3035

Number of cases read: 4   Number of cases listed: 4

PART B:

THE COEFFICIENT OF CONTENT VALIDITY (Ccv) AND THE KAPPA COEFFICIENT, IN THE DETERMINATION OF THE CONTENT VALIDITY, ACCORDING TO THE TECHNIQUE OF PANEL OF EXPERTS

INTRODUCTION

The problem evaluating the ***content validity*** of a given measurement instrument of the type of Likert scale or objective test (multiple choice), in the past was done mainly through the logical and critical analysis of each one of the items of the instrument, by the same author or of by some content experts (Anastasi, 1967, 1982), Thorndike and Hagen, 1970; Nunnally, 1978; Garmines and Zeller, 1979; Hernández-Sampieri, Fernández-Collado and Baptista-Lucio, 1998; Nunnally and Bernstein, 1995).

When the technique of *Panel of Experts* is used to determine the *content validity* of an instrument, the generated data takes the matrix form: I x J (where I = items, J = Judges), in which a scale of k scores is used to evaluate the validity of each one of the items as well as the validity of the total instrument as a whole. Some investigators have used certain statistical procedures to determine the agreement among judges, each one presenting certain limitations. The need arises for *a new coefficient to measure the content validity* of data gathering instruments.

In this work, a new coefficient is proposed: the ***Coefficient of Content Validity (Ccv)***, which permits a *quantitative* approach for measuring and evaluating *content validity.* This coefficient constitutes an extended and more complete version of a preliminary version of the same coefficient presented previously by the author: the ***Coefficient of Proportional Ranges*** (Hernández-Nieto, 1984, 1995).

CHAPTER 1

STATEMENT OF THE PROBLEM

Using the technique of *Experts Panel* to determine the *content validity* and *concordance or agreement* among judges, in relation to certain data-gathering instrument, a data matrix such as this is usually developed:

Items	Judge1	Judge2	....	JudgeJ
1	K_{11}	K_{12}	....	K_{1J}
2	K_{21}	K_{22}	....	K_{2J}
3	K_{31}	K_{32}	....	K_{3J}
...	...	...	....	....
I	K_{I1}	K_{I2}	....	K_{IJ}

Where K_{IJ} represents the score or rank assigned to item Ii by Judge J.

To obtain an specified value, several statistical procedures have been used.

Coefficients used to measure Content Validity and Agreement among Judges

1. - *Coefficient of Pearson Correlation.* Since it requires a continuous scale (either interval or ratio scale), when equality of distances is assumed among the scores of a Likert scale, this coefficient (usually calculated on the average of the correlations of the different pairs among Judges: r_{12}, r_{13}, ... r_{23},

r_{24}....) underestimates the true validity, due to the restricted range of variability among the scores. Also, the correction for ties among scores tends to produce coefficients, which underestimate its real value.

2. - *Coefficient of Spearman Correlation*.

Even when it assumes an ordinal scaling among the scores assigned by each Judge, it has the same limitations of the previous procedure: restricted range and little variability between the score values, resulting in biased underestimation.

3. - *Kappa Coefficient*. To measure the

agreement among different judges about a given number of objects, items or categories, the Kappa coefficient has been used. This coefficient is an estimator of consistency among Judges (interrater reliability) (Fleiss, 1981; Dawson-Saunders and Trapp, 1990). Initially developed for the agreement between two judges, an extended version of this coefficient also exists for *n* objects or items, *m* Judges and *k* scale values (Fleiss, 1981), its calculation is relatively complex given that it requires the use of matrix algebra, suggesting the use of a computer. On the other hand, Kappa only measures the agreement among Judges about a given number of objects or items, but it does not give information about the content validity of an instrument.

Using the method of Panel of Experts, a new algorithm is proposed to obtain a new coefficient which would allow the calculation of *content validity for each item, the content validity for the whole instrument and the level of agreement among judges*: the **Coefficient of Content Validity (Ccv)**.

Compared with the *Kappa Coefficient*, which only measures agreement or concordance among judges, this new coefficient measures both content validity of the instrument and level of agreement two or more judges. The **Ccv** does the calculation from each of the judge's scores on each one of the items or objects (a minimum of 3 and a maximum of 5 judges is recommended). Preferably, the evaluation scale should be between 0 and 5 scores. The **Ccv** is interpreted, according to the following scale:

.00　　.25　　.50　　.75　　1.00

a) Less than .80, *validity* and *concordance* are unacceptable.

b) Equal or greater than .80 and smaller than .90, *validity* and *agreement* are satisfactory.

c) Equal or higher than .90, up to a maximum of 1.00, *validity* and *agreement* are excellent.

The calculation of the **Cvc** is relatively simple and it only requires the use of a manual calculator. However, if many objects or items are involved, for higher speed and versatility in the computation, computer statistical packages such as the **SPSS**

(Statistical Package for the Social the Sciences) (Spss, 1999), should be used.

By means of a set of examples, it is demonstrated that the *Ccv* measures validity and concordance, while the Kappa coefficient only measures *concordance* or *agreement* among judges.

All the calculations for the *Ccv* were carried out using some software programs written in the SPSS regular syntax language. For the computation of the *Kappa Coefficient*, a program in the *matrix language* of SPSS was developed, given that this coefficient requires operations with matrices.

CHAPTER 2

BACKGROUND OF THE PROBLEM. THE

NEEED FOR A NEW COEFFICIENT

The problem of measuring and evaluating the *content validity* of a given instrument, has been generally considered in the psychometric literature as the problem of a *systematic logical analysis of its content* to determine if it constitutes an appropriate sample of what it is supposed to be measuring, especially in the case of achievement tests (Anastasi, 1967, 1982). In other occasions, the *content validity* has consisted of a logical discussion among experts and judges on the convincing arguments by the same author about how pertinent and relevant is the content of the instrument (Magnusson, 1969; Thorndike, 1970; Nunnally, 1978).

A problem related to the *content validity*, is the problem of measuring and evaluating the *agreement* or *concordance* among judges or experts on the subjective evaluation of a certain event or object. It is the typical case, among clinical researchers, to determine the agreement between two specialists about certain clinical diagnosis. In this case, the fundamental problem is to determine the *consistency* among the experts or specialists ("inter-rater reliability", or "consistency"), independently of the valuation per se of the diagnosis under consideration. For this type of situations, the *Kappa*

Coefficient was developed, used initially in 2 x 2 contingency tables, and later extended for any number of objects and judges (Fleiss, 1981).

Antecedents of the Kappa Coefficient

Fleiss (1981) presented a set of indexes, which constitute the antecedents for the development of the *Kappa Coefficient*. From a 2 x 2 contingency table, of the following form:

Table 1
General Structure of a 2x 2 Contingency Table

		Judge B		
		+	-	
Judge A	+	a	b	P_1
	-	c	d	Q_1
		P_2	Q_2	

Where **a, b, c** y **d** are frequencies, and P_1, P_2, Q_1 y Q_2 are proportions.

The indexes presented and discussed by Fleiss are the following :

a) Concordance Index (simplex):

$$p_0 = a + d.$$

b) General Index of Concordance:

$$2 p_0 - 1 = 2 (a+d) - 1$$

Holley and Guilford (1964), Maxwell (1977), in Fleiss (1981).

c.1) Specific Index of Agreement (a).

When the proportion *d* is relatively large, and the agreement is overestimated, it is recommended to ignore to proportion *d*:

$$ps = 2a / (2a+b+c) = a/p$$

where p = (p1 + p2)/2.

Dice (1945), in Fleiss (1981).

c.2) Specific Index of Agreement (b)

When p's is ignored to:

p's = 2d / (2d +b+c) = d/q

where q = 1 - p = 1 - (p1 + p2) /2,

Fleiss (1981).

d) Average Index of ps and p's:

A = ½(ps + p's)

A = a / (p1 + p2) + d / (q1 + q2)

Rogot and Goldberg (1966), in Fleiss (1981).

e) Coefficient Lambda λ_r :

λ_r = [2a - (b+c)] / [2a + (b+c)].

Godman and Kruskal (1954), in Fleiss (1981).

f) *Kappa Coefficient :*

$$K = (Io - Ie) / (1 - Ie)$$

Where *Io* is the Observed Index and *Ie* is the Expected Index. In terms of proportions:

$$K = 2 (ad - bc) / (p1\ q2 + p2\ q1).$$

Fleiss (1981)

Kappa is equivalent to any of the previous indexes (po, ps, p's, A), once the random factor of agreement has been eliminated from each one of them. Equally, it is equivalent to the coefficients of *Intraclass Correlation*, when quantitative scales are used (Ebel, 1951), in Fleiss (1981).

The Coefficient of Content Validity (Ccv)

It is then evident the need for a new coefficient to measure content validity and agreement among judges, at the same time that it should be relatively simple to calculate. The fundamental question to be answered, would be the following:

Which is the magnitude of the observed evaluation score obtained among the judges in comparison with the maximum expected evaluation score (excellent), according to the measuring scale being used ...?

When trying to respond to this question, a new coefficient is proposed, in the following terms:

The **Coefficient of Total Content Validity (Cvc₁)** is defined as the average of the *Coefficients of Content Validity* for each item, each one of which has been corrected for random agreement among judges:

$$\frac{\sum Cvc_{ic}}{N} = \sum \left[\left[\frac{\sum x_i / J}{Vmx} \right] - p_{ei} \right] \left(\frac{1}{N} \right)$$

Where:

N = total number of items of the instrument of the data gathering instrument

$\sum x_i$ = sum of the score values assigned by each judge J to each one of the items I

Vmx = maximum value of the scale used by the judges

p_{ei} = probability of the error for each item (probability of random agreement among judges)

J = Number of Judges assigning evaluation scores to each item

Note: When each one of the judges assigns scores to each one of the items, p_{ei} becomes a constant ($p_{ei} = p_e$) for each one of the items, and therefore, an alternative formula of Ccv_t would be:

$$Cvc_{tc} = \frac{\sum Cvc_i}{N} - p_e$$

Where:

Ccv_i = set of values of the *Coefficient of Content Validity* for each item.

p_e = Estimation of the probability error (when constant for each item)

The ***Coefficient of Content Validity*** for each item *(Ccv_i)*, is defined as the *relative proportion*, in relation to the *maximum value of the scale*, of the average evaluation scores among judges for each item *(Ccv_i)* corrected for random agreement *(p_{ei})*:

$$Cvc_{ic} = \left[\frac{\sum x_i / J}{Vmx} \right] - p_{ei}$$

Where *p_{ei}* is an specific value for each item, when some of the judges do not assign a value to the corresponding item. Otherwise, it is a constant.

Development of the Algorithm:

Be *Mx* = **∑***x_i* */J*; the average of the scores assigned by each judge to each item, where J =

number of Judges. It represents the level of evaluation obtained by each item, among the judges.

Be Ccv_i the *proportional* relationship of Mx in relation to the *maximum value* of the measuring scale (Vmx) used by the judges:

$$Cvc_i = \frac{Mx}{Vmx}$$

Be Ccv_i the proportional relationship of Mx in relation to the maximum value of the measuring scale (Vmx) used by the Judges:

This value indicates the proportional relationship of the observed evaluation level, given by the J judges, in relation to the maximum expected value (excellent evaluation) (Vmx = maximum value of the scale). In other words, it indicates us the proportional relationship among the *overall estimate* of the obtained valuation (*Mx*) among the judges, and the maximum valuation possible (*Vmx*). This is the appropriate response to the fundamental question proposed earlier.

Correction for Random Agreement: Estimation of the Error Probability

The proportional relationship $Ccv_i = Mx / Vmx$, contains some error because, although each judge evaluates independently each item, there is always the probability that one or more judges assign evaluation scores at random, generating a biased estimate of agreement. It is, therefore, necessary to correct this proportional relationship, eliminating the probability of random agreement.

To estimate in each Ccv_i the probability of the random agreement among the scores from the J Judges, we use the binomial distribution:

$$\binom{N}{x} p^x q^{N-x} = \frac{N!}{x!(N-x)!} p^x q^{N-x}$$

(Hays, 1973, p. 184)

Where N is the total number of objects (items, in our case), x is the subset of objects (items) belonging to N, p is the probability success (in our case, agreement) and q is the probability of the failure (non agreement, in our case).

If we assume that $(x = J)$ (the total number of judges is concordant), then:

$$\mathbf{p_e} = \binom{N}{x} p^x q^{N-x} = \frac{N!}{x!(N-x)!} p^x q^{N-x}$$

$$\mathbf{p_e} = \binom{J}{J} p^J q^{J-J} = \frac{J!}{J!(J-J)!} p^J q^0$$

$$\mathbf{p_e} = \frac{J!}{J!(0)!} p^J q^0 = \frac{J!}{J!} \; p^J(1) = p^J \,,$$

$\mathbf{p_e}$ is equal to the probability of success of the J judges (agreement), to the power of J.

Since $p = (1/J)$, by definition of the probability of an event among J objects, then:

$$\boxed{p_e = (1/J)^J}$$

Another demonstration:

The probability that a Judge assigns scores at random, for each item, is equal to: $(1/J)$. If we assume that each one of the Judges is assigning, independently from each other, the corresponding score value to each one of the items, we can calculate the probability of the joint event of the J judges:

$$p \ (J_1 \cap J_2 \cap J_3 \cap \ldots\ldots\ldots J_n) =$$

$$(p \ J_1 \ ) \ x \ (p \ J_2) \ x \ (pJ_3) \ x \ \ldots\ldots (pJ_n) =$$

$$p \ (J_1 \cap J_2 \cap J_3 \cap \ldots\ldots\ldots J_n) =$$

$$(1/J) \ x \ (1/J) \ x \ (1/J) \ x \ \ldots (1/J) = \ \mathbf{(1/J)}^{\ J}$$

Therefore, the ***Coefficient of Content Validity*** for each item ***(Ccv_i)***, *corrected for random agreement*, is equal to the ***Coefficient of Content Validity for each item (Ccv_i)***, *minus* the ***probability of error (p_e)***:

$$Cvc_{ic} = Cvc_i - p_{ei} = Cvc_i - (1 \ / \ J)^J$$

CHAPTER 3

COMPARISONS BETWEEN THE

COEFFICIENT OF CONTENT VALIDITY (Ccv)

AND

THE *KAPPA COEFFICIENT (K)*

The fundamental property of the *Coefficient of Content Validity (Cvc),* when compared to the *Kappa Coefficient (K)*, is not that it measures agreement among judges, but rather that it also measures *content validity* (the property of an instrument of measuring what it intends to measure, according to some experts). By means of some examples, this property can be evidenced.

Calculation of the Coefficient of Content Validity (Ccv) and the Kappa Coefficient (K). Examples

Example 1:

The case of an instrument with ten items, which are evaluated on their *content validity (Ccv Coefficient)* by five judges (Technique of Experts Panel) on a measuring scale of three points (Table 2).

Table 2
Estimation of *Ccv* When a Matrix of Ten (10) Objects (Items) are Evaluated by Five (5) Judges, on a Scale of Three (3) Points. Unacceptable Validity.

It.	\multicolumn{5}{c}{Judges (j)}						
	1	2	3	4	5	$\sum x$	M	Cvc	p_e	Cvc_c
01	1	2	2	2	2	9	1.8	.60	.0032	.5968
02	1	1	3	3	3	11	2.2	.77	.0032	.7668
03	3	3	3	3	3	15	3.0	1.0	.0032	.9968
04	1	1	1	1	3	7	1.4	.47	.0032	.4668
05	1	1	1	3	3	9	1.8	.60	.0032	.5968
06	1	2	2	2	2	9	1.8	.60	.0032	.5968

07	1	1	1	1	1	5	1.0	.33	.0032	.3268
08	2	2	2	2	3	11	2.2	.73	.0032	.7268
09	1	3	3	3	3	13	2.6	.87	.0032	.8868
10	1	1	1	3	3	9	1.8	.60	.0032	.5968

$$Ccv_{tc} = \sum Ccv_{ic} / 10 = 6.558 / 10 = .6558$$

Unacceptable Validity.

Alternatively, when p_e is a constant:

$$Ccv_t = \sum Ccv_i / 10 = 6.570 / 10 = .6570$$

$$pe = .0032$$

$$Ccv_{tc} = .65700 - .0032 = .65668$$

The obtained *marginal difference* (.65680 - .65668 = .00012) is due to the decimal differences, for over or under estimations, which always occur when the constant p_e is subtracted from each one of the values of the non-corrected Ccv_i.

Where:

$\sum x_{ij}$ = sum of all the scores assigned by the Judges to each item.

M_x = mean of the scores = $\sum x_{ij}$ / **J**; where **J** = number of Judges

Ccv_i = *Coefficient of Content Validity* for each one of the items.

p_{ei} = random probability of concordance or agreement among the Judges.

$Ccvt_c$ is the *Coefficient of Corrected Total Content Validity*

Example 2:

Evaluation of ten items by three judges, on a scale of three points. *Acceptable Concordance. Calculation of Kappa* (Table 3).

Table 3:
Estimation of Kappa When a Matrix of Ten (10) Objects (Items) is Evaluated by Five (5) Judges, on a Scale of Three (3) Points. Acceptable Concordance.

Items	*Scores*			Σx_{ij}	Σx_{ij}^2
	1	*2*	*3*		
01	1	4	0	5	17
02	2	0	3	5	13
03	0	0	5	5	25
04	4	0	1	5	17
05	3	0	2	5	13
06	1	4	0	5	17
07	5	0	0	5	25
08	0	4	1	5	17
09	1	0	4	5	17
10	3	0	2	5	13
Total	**20**	**12**	**18**	-	**174**

Kappa for each scale score j = 1, 2 3.

$$Kappa_j = 1 - [\Sigma \, X_{ij} \, (m - X_{ij}) \, / \, nm \, (m\text{-}1) \, (p_j \, q_j)]$$

Where:

X_{ij} = score frequencies (on a scale of 1 to 3, in this case) given by the five (5) judges

m = the number o judges

n = number of objects or items

k = number of scale points

p_j = total proportion for each score or rank
j = 1, 2, ..., k

q_j = 1 - p_j, complement of p_j

Notice that the sum of the corresponding frequencies $(\sum x_i)$ *is always equal* to 5 (the number of judges, in this example).

Total Kappa (K_t):

$$K_t = 1 - [(nm^2 - \sum \sum X^2_{ij}) / nm \, (m-1) \, (\sum p_i \, q_j \,)]$$

(Fleiss, 1981, p. 230)

$K_1 = .29$ (score 1); $K_2 = .67$ (score 2);

$K_3 = .35$ (score 3)

$K_t = .42$ *(Acceptable Concordance)*

To evaluate the obtained value of *Kappa* (total or specific), the following scale is used:

$.76 \leq$ *Kappa* ≤ 1.00 ------ excellent
$.41 \leq$ *Kappa* $\leq .75$ ------ satisfactory
$-1.00 \leq$ *Kappa* $\leq .40$ ----- unsatisfactory

Example 3:

Evaluation of ten items by three judges on a scale

of three points. *Perfect Concordance. Unacceptable*

Validity (Table 4).

Table 4
Estimation of Coefficients Ccv and Kappa When a Matrix of
Ten (10) Objects (items) are Evaluated by Five (5) Judges, on
a Scale of Three (3) Points. Unacceptable Validity. Perfect
Concordance on Score 1.

It	Judges (j)					$\sum$	M	Ccv	p_e	Ccv_c
	1	2	3	4	5					
01	1	1	1	1	1	5	1	.33	.0032	.596
02	1	1	1	1	1	5	1	.33	.0032	.766
03	1	1	1	1	1	5	1	.33	.0032	.996
04	1	1	1	1	1	5	1	.33	.0032	.466
05	1	1	1	1	1	5	1	.33	.0032	.596
06	1	1	1	1	1	5	1	.33	.0032	.596
07	1	1	1	1	1	5	1	.33	.0032	.326
08	1	1	1	1	1	5	1	.33	.0032	.726
09	1	1	1	1	1	5	1	.33	.0032	.886
10	1	1	1	1	1	5	1	.33	.0032	.596

K_1= 1.0 (score 1)
K_2 = non computable (score 2)
K_3 = non computable (score 3)

K_t= 1.0 (total) *(Perfect Total Concordance)*

Ccv_t = 0.33300

$p_e = 0.00032$ *(constant)*
$Ccv_{tc} = 0.33268$ *(Unacceptable Validity)*

Perfect Consistency, Unacceptable Validity

Example 4:

Evaluation of ten items by five judges, on a scale of three points. *Perfect Concordance. Unacceptable validity* (Table 5).

Table 5
Estimation of Coefficients Cvc and Kappa When a Matrix of Ten (10) Objects (Items) is Evaluated by Five (5) Judges on a Scale of Three (3) Points. Unacceptable Validity. Perfect Concordance on Score 2.

It	Judges (j)					Σ	M	Ccv	p_e	Ccv_c
	1	2	3	4	5					
01	2	2	2	2	2	10	2	.663	.0032	.6626
02	2	2	2	2	2	10	2	.663	.0032	.6626
03	2	2	2	2	2	10	2	.663	.0032	.6626
04	2	2	2	2	2	10	2	.663	.0032	.6626
05	2	2	2	2	2	10	2	.663	.0032	.6626
06	2	2	2	2	2	10	2	.663	.0032	.6626
07	2	2	2	2	2	10	2	.663	.0032	.6626
08	2	2	2	2	2	10	2	.663	.0032	.6626
09	2	2	2	2	2	10	2	.663	.0032	.6626
10	2	2	2	2	2	10	2	.663	.0032	.6626

K_1 = non computable (score 1)
K_2 = 1.0 (score 2)
K_3 = non computable (score 3)

K_t = 1.0 (total) **(Perfect Total Concordance)**

Cvc_t = 0.66300
p_e = 0.00032 (constant)
Cvc_{tc} = 0.66268 (Unacceptable Validity)

<u>Perfect Concordance, Unacceptable Validity</u>

Example 5:

Evaluation of ten items by five judges on a scale

of three points. *Perfect concordance. Perfect validity*

(Table 6).

Table 6
**Estimation of Coefficients Cvc and Kappa When a Matrix
of Ten (10) Objects (Items) is Evaluated by Five (5) Judges,
on a Scale of Three (3) Points. Perfect Concordance on
Score 3. Perfect Validity.**

It.	Judges (j)					Σ	M	Ccv	p_e	Ccv_c
	1	2	3	4	5					
01	3	3	3	3	3	15	3	1	.0032	.9996
02	3	3	3	3	3	15	3	1	.0032	.9996
03	3	3	3	3	3	15	3	1	.0032	.9996
04	3	3	3	3	3	15	3	1	.0032	.9996

05	3	3	3	3	3	15	3	1	.0032	.9996
06	3	3	3	3	3	15	3	1	.0032	.9996
07	3	3	3	3	3	15	3	1	.0032	.9996
08	3	3	3	3	3	15	3	1	.0032	.9996
09	3	3	3	3	3	15	3	1	.0032	.9996
10	3	3	3	3	3	15	3	1	.0032	.9996

$Cvc_t = 1.00000$
$p_e = 0.00032$ *(constant)*
$Cvc_{tc} = 0.99968$ *(Perfect Validity)*

K_1 = non computable (score 1)
K_2 = non computable (score 2)
K_3 = 1.00 (score 3)

$K_t = 1.0$ (total) **(Perfect Total Concordance).**

Perfect Concordance, Perfect Validity

Example 6:

Estimation of the *Ccv* when the measuring scale is of five scores. *Unacceptable Validity* (Table 7).

Table 7
Estimation of the Ccv When a Matrix of Ten (10) Objects (Items) is Evaluated by Five (5) Judges, on Scale of Five (5) Scores. Unacceptable Validity.

It	Judges (j)					Σ	M	Cvc	p_e	Cvc_c
	1	2	3	4	5					
01	1	3	4	5	2	15	3.0	.60	.0032	.6916

02	1	2	4	5	5	17	3.4	.68	.0032	.6916
03	3	3	3	3	3	15	3.0	.60	.0032	.6916
04	4	4	4	4	4	20	4.0	.80	.0032	.6916
05	3	4	5	4	4	20	4.0	.80	.0032	.6916
06	1	3	4	5	4	17	3.4	.68	.0032	.6916
07	1	3	4	5	5	18	3.6	.72	.0032	.6916
08	5	3	2	4	4	18	3.6	.72	.0032	.6916
09	4	5	5	5	4	13	2.6	.52	.0032	.6916
10	3	4	5	4	4	20	4.0	.80	.0032	.6916

$Cvc_t = 0.69200$
$p_e = 0.00032$ *(constant)*
$Cvc_{tc} = 0.69168.$

Unacceptable Validity

Example 7:

Calculation of *Kappa* when evaluating ten items by five judges, on a scale of five points (Table 8).

Table 8
Estimation of Kappa When a Matrix of Ten (10) Objects (Items) is Evaluated by Five (5) Judges, in a Scale of Five (5) Points. Absence of Concordance.

| Items | Scores | | | | | Σx_{ij} | Σx_{ij}^2 |
	1	2	3	4	5		
01	1	1	1	1	1	5	5

02	1	1	0	1	2	5	7
03	0	0	5	0	0	5	25
04	0	0	0	5	0	5	25
05	0	0	1	3	1	5	11
06	1	0	1	2	1	5	7
07	1	0	1	1	2	5	7
08	0	1	1	2	1	5	7
09	0	0	0	2	3	5	13
10	0	0	1	3	1	5	11
Total	**4**	**3**	**11**	**20**	**12**		**118**

$K_1 = -.086$ (score 1)
$K_2 = -.064$ (score 2)
$K_3 = .301$ (score 3)
$K_4 = .120$ (score 4)
$K_5 = -.040$ (score 5)

$K_t = -.0884$ (total)

Absence of Total Concordance

Example 8:

Evaluation of ten items by five judges on a scale of five points. Calculation of *Coefficients Ccv* and *Kappa. Perfect concordance. Unacceptable validity* (Table 9).

Table 9
Estimation of the Coefficients Cvc and Kappa When a Matrix of Ten (10) Objects (Items) is Evaluated by Five (5) Judges, on a Scale of Five (5) Points. Perfect Concordance on Score 1. Unacceptable Validity

It.	Judges (j)					Σ	M	Ccv	p_e	Ccv_c
	1	2	3	4	5					
01	1	1	1	1	1	5	1	.20	.0032	.1968
02	1	1	1	1	1	5	1	.20	.0032	.1968
03	1	1	1	1	1	5	1	.20	.0032	.1968
04	1	1	1	1	1	5	1	.20	.0032	.1968
05	1	1	1	1	1	5	1	.20	.0032	.1968
06	1	1	1	1	1	5	1	.20	.0032	.1968
07	1	1	1	1	1	5	1	.20	.0032	.1968
08	1	1	1	1	1	5	1	.20	.0032	.1968
09	1	1	1	1	1	5	1	.20	.0032	.1968
10	1	1	1	1	1	5	1	.20	.0032	.1968

$Ccv_t = 0.2000$
$p_e = 0.0032$ (constant)
$Ccv_{tc} = 0.1968$ (Unacceptable Validity)

$K_1 = 1.0$ (score 1)
$K_2 =$ non computable (score 2)
$K_3 =$ non computable (score 3)
$K_4 =$ non computable (score 4)
$K_5 =$ non computable (score 5)

K_t $= 1.000$ (total) **(Perfect Total Concordance)**

Perfect Concordance, Unacceptable Validity

Example 9:

Evaluation of ten items by five judges on a

scale of five points. Calculation of Coefficients Ccv

and Kappa. *Perfect Concordance. Unacceptable*

validity (Table 10).

Table 10
**Estimation of the Coefficients Cvc and Kappa When a Matrix
of Ten (10) Objects (Items) is Evaluated by Five (5) Judges,
on a Scale of Five (5) Points. Perfect Agreement on Score 2.
Unacceptable Validity**

It.	Judges (j)					Σ	M	Ccv	p_e	Ccv_c
	1	2	3	4	5					
01	2	2	2	2	2	10	2	.40	.0032	.3996
02	2	2	2	2	2	10	2	.40	.0032	.3996
03	2	2	2	2	2	10	2	.40	.0032	.3996
04	2	2	2	2	2	10	2	.40	.0032	.3996
05	2	2	2	2	2	10	2	.40	.0032	.3996
06	2	2	2	2	2	10	2	.40	.0032	.3996
07	2	2	2	2	2	10	2	.40	.0032	.3996
08	2	2	2	2	2	10	2	.40	.0032	.3996
09	2	2	2	2	2	10	2	.40	.0032	.39968
10	2	2	2	2	2	10	2	.40	.0032	.39968

*$Ccv_t = 0.40000$; $p_e = 0.00032$ (constant); $Ccv_{tc} = 0.39968$;
(Unacceptable Validity)*

K_1 = non computable (score 1)

$K_2 = 1.0$ (score 2)
K_3 = non computable (score 3)
K_4 = non computable (score 4)
K_5 = non computable (score 5)

$K_t = 1.0$ (total) **(Total Perfect Concordance)**

Perfect Concordance, Unacceptable Validity

Example 10:

Evaluation of ten items by five judges on a scale of five points. Estimation of *Ccv* and *Kappa*. *Perfect concordance. Unacceptable Validity* (Table 11).

Table 11
Estimation of the Coefficients Cvc and Kappa When a Matrix of Ten (10) Objects (Items) is Evaluated by Five (5) Judges, on a Scale of Five (5) Points. Perfect Concordance on Score 3. Unacceptable Validity

It	Jueces (j)					Σx	M	Ccv	p_e	Cvc_c
	1	2	3	4	5					
01	3	3	3	3	3	15	3	.60	.0032	.59968
02	3	3	3	3	3	15	3	.60	.0032	.59968
03	3	3	3	3	3	15	3	.60	.0032	.59968
04	3	3	3	3	3	15	3	.60	.0032	.59968
05	3	3	3	3	3	15	3	.60	.0032	.59968

06	3	3	3	3	3	15	3	.60	.0032	.59968
07	3	3	3	3	3	15	3	.60	.0032	.59968
08	3	3	3	3	3	15	3	.60	.0032	.59968
09	3	3	3	3	3	15	3	.60	.0032	.59968
10	3	3	3	3	3	15	3	.60	.0032	.59968

K_1 = non computable (score 1)
K_2 = non computable (score 2)
K_3 = 1.0 (score 3)
K_4 = non computable (score 4)
K_5 = non computable (score 5)

K_t = 1.00 (total) **(Perfect Total Concordance).**

$Ccv_t = 0.6000$
$p_e = 0.0032$ *(constant)*
$Ccv_{tc} = 0.5968$ *(Unacceptable Validity)*

Perfect Concordance, Unacceptable Validity

Example 11:

Evaluation of ten items by five judges on a scale of five points. Estimation of Cvc and Kappa. *Perfect concordance. Acceptable validity* (Table 12).

Table 12
Estimation of Coefficients Cvc and Kappa When a Matrix of Ten (10) Objects (Items) is Evaluated by Five (5) Judges, on a Scale of Five (5) Points. Perfect Concordance on Score 4. Acceptable Validity

| It | Judges (j) | | | | | $\sum x$ | M | Cvc | p_e | Cvc_c |
	1	2	3	4	5					
01	4	4	4	4	4	20	4	.80	.0032	.79968
02	4	4	4	4	4	20	4	.80	.0032	.79968
03	4	4	4	4	4	20	4	.80	.0032	.79968
04	4	4	4	4	4	20	4	.80	.0032	.79968
05	4	4	4	4	4	20	4	.80	.0032	.79968
06	4	4	4	4	4	20	4	.80	.0032	.79968
07	4	4	4	4	4	20	4	.80	.0032	.79968
08	4	4	4	4	4	20	4	.80	.0032	.79968
09	4	4	4	4	4	20	4	.80	.0032	.79968
10	4	4	4	4	4	20	4	.80	.0032	.79968

K_1 = non computable (score 1)
K_2 = non computable (score 2)
K_3 = non computable (score 3)
K_4 = 1.0 (score 4)
K_5 = non computable (score 5)

K_t = 1.0 (total)   **(Perfect Total Concordance)**

$Ccv_t = 0.8000$
$p_e = 0.0032$ *(constant)*
$Ccv_{tc} = 0.7968$ *(Acceptable Validity)*

Perfect Concordance, Acceptable Validity

Example 12:

Evaluation of ten items by five judges on a scale of five points. Estimation of Coefficients ***Ccv*** and ***Kappa***. *Perfect concordance. Perfect validity* (Table 13).

Table 13
Estimation of Coefficients Cvc and Kappa When a Matrix of Ten (10) Objects (Items) is Evaluated by Five (5) Judges, on a Scale of Five (5) Points. Perfect Concordance on Score 5. Perfect Validity.

It.	Judges (j)					$\sum x$	M	Ccv	p_e	Ccv_c
	1	2	3	4	5					
01	5	5	5	5	5	25	5	1	.0032	.9996
02	5	5	5	5	5	25	5	1	.0032	.9996
03	5	5	5	5	5	25	5	1	.0032	.9996
04	5	5	5	5	5	25	5	1	.0032	.9996
05	5	5	5	5	5	25	5	1	.0032	.9996
06	5	5	5	5	5	25	5	1	.0032	.9996
07	5	5	5	5	5	25	5	1	.0032	.9996
08	5	5	5	5	5	25	5	1	.0032	.9996
09	5	5	5	5	5	25	5	1	.0032	.99968
10	5	5	5	5	5	25	5	1	.0032	.99968

K_1 = non computable (score 1)
K_2 = no computable (score 2)
K_3 = non computable (score 3)
K_4 = non computable (score 4)
K_5 = 1.0 (score 5)

K_t = 1.0 (total)

Ccv_t= *1.0000*
p_e = *0.0032 (constant)*
Ccv_{tc} = *0.9968 (Perfect Validity)*

Perfect Concordance, Perfect Validity

In summary, it has been sufficiently demonstrated that *Kappa* measures only *agreement among judges*, but it does not measure *content validity*. The *Ccv* measures *agreement* and *content validity*. The two coefficients coincide in their values only when there is agreement among the judges at the upper level of the measuring scale being used (Table 14).

Table 14

Summary of Tables 1 to Table 13. Consistencies and Inconsistencies Between Kappa and Ccv

Di.	1	2	3	4	5	E	Cvc	Cvc$_c$	K	C	V
A	1	1	1	1	1	3	.333	.332	1	P	U
B	2	2	2	2	2	3	.663	.662	1	P	U
C	3	3	3	3	3	3	1.00	.999	1	P	P
D	1	1	1	1	1	5	.200	.199	1	P	U
E	2	2	2	2	2	5	.400	.399	1	P	U
F	3	3	3	3	3	5	.600	.599	1	P	U
G	4	4	4	4	4	5	.800	.799	1	P	A
G	5	5	5	5	5	5	1.00	.999	1	P	P

Judges (j) spans columns 1 2 3 4 5.

Where:

K = Kappa; C = Concordance
V = Validity
P = Perfect; U = Unacceptable
A = Acceptable

According to Table 14 (Figure 1), it becomes evident that even if there is a *perfect concordance among judges*, it is not a sufficient condition for the existence of a ***perfect or acceptable validity.***

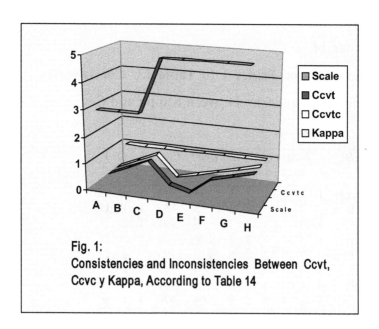

Fig. 1:
Consistencies and Inconsistencies Between Ccvt, Ccvc y Kappa, According to Table 14

CHAPTER 4

CONCLUSION: DIFFERENCES AND SIMILARITIES

As a general conclusion, we can point out the following *differences* and *similarities* between Ccv and Kappa (Table 15):

Table 15:
Differences and Similarities between the *Coefficient of Content Validity (Ccv)* **and the** *Kappa Coefficient (K)*

Kappa	*Ccv*
It only measures Concordance	It measures *simultaneously* Concordance and Validity, within the range .80 ≤ *Cvc* ≤ 1.00
It *does not measure* Content Validity	*It does measure* Content Validity
The range of values oscillates between -1.00 y +1.00	The range of values oscillates between 0.0 y 1.00, when the measuring scale is from 0

Kappa	*Ccv*
	to 5 points. When the measuring scale is from 1 to 3 points, the range oscillates between .33 y 1.00.
The lowest acceptable value is .40, indicating only Concordance.	The lowest acceptable value is .80, indicating both Concordance and Content Validity.
Relatively complex to calculate, when the number of Objects (Items) and of Judges or Experts is large	Relatively easy to calculate, *even* when the number of Objects (Items) and of Judges or Experts is large
The random variation factor is calculated from the total matrix of Objects (Items) x Judges	The random variation factor is calculated from the *vectors of each* Object (Items) x Judges, and from the entire matrix as a whole
The coefficient can be calculated for each one of the scores of the measuring scale (Specific Kappas) as well as for the entire matrix (Total Kappa)	This coefficient determines the content validity for each of the Objects (Items) and for the whole instrument in general, facilitating its depuration
Unless the corresponding matrix is examined, there is no way to determine content validity	It is not necessary to look into the matrix, to be able to determine content validity

REFERENCES

Anastasi, A. (1967). **Tests psicológicos.** (Trad. C.R. Hernández y A. Alvarez Villar). Madrid, España : Aguilar.

Anastasi, A. (1982). **Psychological testing.** (fifth ed.). New York: McMillan

Dawson-Saunders, B. and Trapp, R. G. (1990). **Basic and clinical biostatistics.** Norwalk, Connecticut: Appleton & Lange.

Ebel, R.(1951). Estimation of the reliability of ratings. **Psychometrika, 16,** 407- 424.

Fleiss, J.L. (1981**). Statistical methods for rates and proportions.** (2nd. edition). New York: Wiley.

Garmines, E. G. and Zeller, R.A. (1979). **Reliability and validity assessment**.(Series: Quantitative Applications in the Social Sciences). Beverly Hills, California: Sage University Paper.

Hays, W. (1973). **Statistics for the social sciences**. (Second edition). New York : Holt Rinehart and Winston.

Hernández-Nieto, R.A. (1984**). El Coeficiente de Proporción de Rangos (Cpr): Una alternativa**

para medir la validez de contenido en instrumentos de medición. Trabajo presentado en la XLIV Convención Anual de Asovac. Coro, Edo. Falcón (Venezuela): 13 al 18 de Noviembre.

Hernández-Nieto, R.A. (1995). **El Coeficiente de Proporción de Rangos (Cpr): una alternativa para determinar la validez de contenido y el nivel de concordancia entre jueces en escalas Likert.** Trabajo presentado en el XXV Congreso Interamericano de Psicología. San Juan, Puerto Rico: 9 al 14 de Julio.

Hernández-Urdaneta, R. A. (1995). **Programa de Spss en Lenguaje Matrix para el Cálculo del Coeficiente KAPPA.** Manuscrito no publicado. Mérida, Venezuela: Universidad de Los Andes (Facultad de Ingeniería).

Hernández Nieto, R.A. (1997). **El Coeficiente de Validez de Contenido (Cvc) y el Coeficiente Kappa en la Determinación de la Validez de Contenido de Instrumentos de Recolección de Datos.** Manuscrito no publicado. Mérida, Venezuela: Universidad de Los Andes (Facultad de Humanidades y Educación, Maestría en Educación, Mención Informática y Diseño Instruccional).

Hernández Nieto, R.A. (2000). **El Coeficiente de Validez de Contenido (Cvc) y el Coeficiente Kappa en la Determinación de la Validez de Contenido de Instrumentos de Recolección de**

Datos. Manuscrito no publicado. Mérida, Venezuela: Universidad de Los Andes (Facultad de Ciencias Jurídicas y Políticas, Postgrado en Ciencias Políticas).

Hernández Nieto, R. A. (2001). **Contribuciones al análisis estadístico.** Mérida, Venezuela: Coedición de la Universidad de Los Andes (Facultad de Ciencias Jurídicas, Políticas y Criminológicas) y IESINFO (Instituto de Estudios en Informática). Available thru Greatunpublished.com booksurge.com and Amazon.com

Hernández-Sampieri, R., Fernández-Collado, C., y Baptista-Lucio, P. (1998). **Metodología de la investigación.** México: Mc Graw Hill.

Lilienfeld, A. M. and Lilienfeld, D.E. (1980). **Foundations of epidemiology.** New York: Oxford University Press.

Magnusson, D. (1969). **Teoría de los tests.** (Trad. J. Aguilar). México: Editorial Trillas. (Original en Inglés, 1967).

Nunnally, J. C. (1978). **Psychometric theory.** (Second edition). New York: McGraw Hill Book Co.

Nunnally, J. C. y Bernstein, I. J. (1995). **Teoría psicométrica.** (Tercera edición). (Trad. J.A. Velásquez Arellano). México: McGraw Hill.

SPSS (1999). **SPSS Base 9.0. Applications guide.** Chicago, Illinois: Spss Inc.

Thorndike, R. L y Hagen, E. (1970). **Tests y técnicas de medición en psicología y educación.** (Trad. F.G. Aramburu). México: Editorial Trillas. (Original en Inglés, 1969).

APPENDIXES

DATA FILE FOR THE CALCULATION OF

Ccv

Item	Judge1	Judge2	Judge3
1	5,00	4,00	4,00
2	5,00	4,00	5,00
3	5,00	4,00	4,00
4	5,00	4,00	3,00
5	5,00	4,00	5,00
6	5,00	4,00	4,00
7	5,00	4,00	4,00
8	5,00	5,00	5,00
9	5,00	5,00	5,00
10	5,00	4,00	4,00
11	5,00	4,00	5,00
12	5,00	5,00	5,00
13	5,00	4,00	4,00
14	5,00	5,00	4,00
15	5,00	3,00	4,00
16	5,00	5,00	4,00
17	5,00	5,00	4,00
18	5,00	5,00	5,00
19	5,00	5,00	4,00
20	5,00	5,00	4,00
21	5,00	5,00	5,00
22	5,00	5,00	5,00
23	5,00	4,00	4,00
24	5,00	5,00	4,00
25	5,00	4,00	5,00
26	5,00	4,00	5,00
27	5,00	5,00	5,00
28	5,00	5,00	5,00
29	5,00	4,00	4,00
30	5,00	5,00	4,00
31	5,00	3,00	3,00
32	5,00	5,00	5,00

PROGRAM IN SPSS FOR THE CALCULATION OF Ccv

TITLE 'COEFFICIENT OF CONTENT VALIDITY : Ccv'.
SUBTITLE '(HERNÁNDEZ NIETO, 1994, 1995, 1996, 2000). SPSS
WINDOWS 9.0'.
* SCALE PARTITION:.
 COMPUTE test = 1 .
 EXECUTE .
*** .
* SCALE: FROM 0 TO 5 POINTS:
* 0 ------------------------- 2.5 --------------------------- 5.
* MINIMUM VALUE = 0 (UNACEPTABLE).
* MAXIMUM VALUE = 5 (EXCELENT).
* CRÍTICAL VALUE = 2.5 (UNDEFINED).
***.
* MAXIMUM SCORE :.
 COMPUTE maxvalue = 5 .
 EXECUTE .
* NUMBER OF JUDGES:.
 COMPUTE njudges = 3.
* AVERAGE SCORE AMONG JUDGES:.
 COMPUTE meanjudg = (judge1 + judge2 + judge3) / njudges.
 EXECUTE .
* CALCULATING ERROR FOR EACH ITEM:.
 COMPUTE erroritm = (1/ meanjudg)**njueces.
* CALCULATING VALIDITY FOR EACH ITEM:.
 COMPUTE validitm = (meanjudg / maxalue) - erroritm .
 EXECUTE .
 AGGREGATE
 /OUTFILE='A:\Ccv.SAV'
 /BREAK=test
 /Ccvt 'COEFFICIENT OF TOTAL CONTENT VALIDITY' =
 MEAN(validitm)
 /errort 'probability of total error' = MEAN(erroritm).
* PRINTING FORMATS:.
 PRINT FORMAT PROJUEZ VALIDITM ERRORITM (F5.4).
* LISTING VARIABLES:.
 LIST item judge1 judge2 judge3 meanjudg validitm erroritm.
 GET
 FILE = 'A:\Cvc.SAV'.
* CALCULATING Ccvc (COEF. OF CORRECTED CONTENT
 VALIDITY).
 COMPUTE Ccvc = Ccvt - errort.
* LABELING Ccvc:.
 Variable label Ccvc 'Ccv corrected'.
* PRINTING FORMATS:.
 PRINT FORMAT Ccvt Ccvc errort (F5.4).
* LISTING OF VARIABLES:.
 LIST Ccvt Ccvc errort.

OUTPUT FROM THE SPSS PROGRAM TO CALCULATE THE Ccv
(HERNÁNDEZ NIETO, 1994, 1995, 1996, 2000). SPSS WINDOWS 9.0

ITEM	JUDGE1	JUDGE2	JUDGE3	MEANJUDG	VALIDITM	ERRORITM
1	5,0	4,0	4,0	4,333	,8296	,0370
2	5,0	4,0	5,0	4,667	,8963	,0370
3	5,0	4,0	4,0	4,333	,8296	,0370
4	5,0	4,0	3,0	4,000	,7630	,0370
5	5,0	4,0	5,0	4,667	,8963	,0370
6	5,0	4,0	4,0	4,333	,8296	,0370
7	5,0	4,0	4,0	4,333	,8296	,0370
8	5,0	5,0	5,0	5,000	,9630	,0370
9	5,0	5,0	5,0	5,000	,9630	,0370
10	5,0	4,0	4,0	4,333	,8296	,0370
11	5,0	4,0	5,0	4,667	,8963	,0370
12	5,0	5,0	5,0	5,000	,9630	,0370
13	5,0	4,0	4,0	4,333	,8296	,0370
14	5,0	5,0	4,0	4,667	,8963	,0370
15	5,0	3,0	4,0	4,000	,7630	,0370
16	5,0	5,0	4,0	4,667	,8963	,0370
17	5,0	5,0	4,0	4,667	,8963	,0370
18	5,0	5,0	5,0	5,000	,9630	,0370
19	5,0	5,0	4,0	4,667	,8963	,0370
20	5,0	5,0	4,0	4,667	,8963	,0370
21	5,0	5,0	5,0	5,000	,9630	,0370
22	5,0	5,0	5,0	5,000	,9630	,0370
23	5,0	4,0	4,0	4,333	,8296	,0370
24	5,0	5,0	4,0	4,667	,8963	,0370
25	5,0	4,0	5,0	4,667	,8963	,0370
26	5,0	4,0	5,0	4,667	,8963	,0370
27	5,0	5,0	5,0	5,000	,9630	,0370
28	5,0	5,0	5,0	5,000	,9630	,0370
29	5,0	4,0	4,0	4,333	,8296	,0370
30	5,0	5,0	4,0	4,667	,8963	,0370
31	5,0	3,0	3,0	3,667	,6963	,0370
32	5,0	5,0	5,0	5,000	,9630	,0370

CCVT	CCVC	ERRORT
,8838	,8468	,0370

PROGRAM IN SPSS MATRIX LANGUAGE TO CALCULATE THE Ccv

*AUTHOR: Eng.. Rafael A. Hernández-Urdaneta (1995)

```
DATA LIST FREE/OBJECT  PT01 PT02 PT03 PT04
PT05.
BEGIN DATA.
1 1 2 2 2 2
2 1 1 3 3 3
3 3 3 3 3 3
4 1 1 1 1 3
5 1 1 1 3 3
6 1 2 2 2 2
7 1 1 1 1 1
8 2 2 2 2 3
9 1 3 3 3 3
10 1 1 1 3 3
END DATA.
MATRIX.
GET A /VARIABLES=PT01 PT02 PT03 PT04 PT05. /*
scores assigned by each judge */
COMPUTE N=NROW(A). /* n objects or items */
COMPUTE M=NCOL(A). /* number of  judges */
COMPUTE J=MMAX(A).
COMPUTE C=1+RSUM(A)-RSUM(A).
COMPUTE  CVCI=RSUM(A)/(M*J).
COMPUTE PE=(1/(M**M)).
COMPUTE Q=PE*C.
COMPUTE CVCIC=CSUM(CVCI-Q)/N.
COMPUTE CVCTC= CVCIC-PE.
PRINT PE/FORMAT=F12.5 /TITLE 'Pe "probability of
random concordance for each item"'.
PRINT CCVI/FORMAT=F12.2 /TITLE 'CCVic "CCV for
each corrected item" ' .
PRINT CCVTC/FORMAT=F12.2 /TITLE 'CCVtc "CCV
Corrected Total" ' .
END MATRIX.
```

OUTPUT FROM THE SPSS MATRIX PROGRAM TO CALCULATE THE Ccv

Matrix

Run MATRIX procedure:

Pe ´probability of random concordance for each item´   ,00032

CVCic ´CCV for each corrected item´

                ,60
                ,73
            1,00
                ,47
                ,60
                ,60
                ,33
                ,73
                ,87
                ,60

CVCtc ´CCV Corrected Total' .
                ,65

------ END MATRIX -----

EXAMPLE OF DATA BASE TO CALCULATE
THE KAPPA COEFFICIENT
(TABLE 3)

Items	Scores		
	1	*2*	*3*
01	1	4	0
02	2	0	3
03	0	0	5
04	4	0	1
05	3	0	2
06	1	4	0
07	5	0	0
08	0	4	1
09	1	0	4
10	3	0	2

PROGRAM IN SPSS MATRIX LANGUAGE TO CALCULATE THE KAPPA COEFFICIENT

Author: Eng. Rafael Hernández Urdaneta (1995)

```
TITLE: 'PROGRAM IN SPSS MATRIX
LANGUAGE TO CALCULATE  KAPPA'.
SUBTITLE: 'AUTHOR: ENG. RAFAEL
HERNÁNDEZ-URDANETA (1995)'.

MATRIX.
GET A /FILE='C:\KAPPA.SAV'.  /* data file for
kappa */
COMPUTE N=NROW(A). /* n subjects */
COMPUTE M=RSUM(A(1,:)). /* m raters */
COMPUTE K=NCOL(A).  /* k categories */
COMPUTE R=RSSQ(A).
COMPUTE C=CSUM(A).
COMPUTE C1=RSUM(C).
COMPUTE C2=CSUM(R).
COMPUTE P=C/C1.
COMPUTE Q=1-P.
COMPUTE L=P*T(Q).
COMPUTE Y=C-C.
COMPUTE KJ=T(Y).
COMPUTE X=0.
LOOP J=1 TO K.
   LOOP I= 1 TO N.
     COMPUTE Y(J)=Y(J)+A(I,J)*(M-A(I,J)).
   END LOOP.
 COMPUTE X=X+(P(J)*Q(J)*(Q(J)-P(J))).
```

```
 COMPUTE KJ(J)=1-(Y(J)/(N*M*(M-
1)*P(J)*Q(J))).
END LOOP.
COMPUTE KAPPA=1-((N*RSSQ(M)-
C2)/(N*M*(M-1)*L)).
COMPUTE S=(SQRT(2)/(L*SQRT(N*M*(M-
1))))*(SQRT(RSSQ(L)-X)).
COMPUTE SJ=SQRT(2/(N*M*(M-1))).
PRINT KJ /FORMAT=F12.2 /TITLE='Kappa for
"J" categories (^Kj)'.
PRINT SJ /FORMAT=F12.3 /TITLE='Std Error
for "J" categories  s.e.o(^Kj)'.
PRINT S /FORMAT=F12.3 /TITLE= 'Std Error
"Overall Kappa" s.e.o(^K)'.
PRINT KAPPA /FORMAT=F12.2
/TITLE='Overall Kappa (^K)'.
END MATRIX.
```

OUTPUT FROM THE SPSS MATRIX LANGUAGE PROGRAM TO CALCULATE THE KAPPA COEFFICIENT

(Data from Table 3)

: 'PROGRAM IN SPSS MATRIX LANGUAGE TO CALCULATE KAPPA'
: 'AUTHOR: ENG. RAFAEL HERNÁNDEZ-URDANETA (1995)'

Matrix

```
Run MATRIX procedure:

Kappa for "J" categories (^Kj)
          ,29
          ,67
          ,35

Std Error for "J" categories  s.e.o(^Kj)
        ,100

Std Error   "Overall Kappa" s.e.o(^K)
        ,072

Overall Kappa (^K)
          ,42

------ END MATRIX -----
```

AUTHORS AND CONTENT INDEX

GLOSARY OF TERMS

C

CMDND (Coefficient of Median Deviation):
Ratio between the Median Deviation and the Median

CMD (Coefficient of Mean Deviation): Ratio between the Mean Deviation and the Mean

CR (Coefficient of Rank or Coefficient of Relative Variability): Ratio between the Range and the midpoint of the difference between the maximum and minimum values

CV (Coefficient o Variance): Ratio between the Standard Deviation and the Arithmetic Mean

CQV (Coeficient of Quartile Variance): Ratio between the Quartile Deviation and the midpoint between Quartile 3 and Quartile 1

Coefficient of Content Validity (Ccv) : Relative proportion, in relation to the maximum value of the measuring scale, of the average score among the judges for each of the items

Coefficient of Proporcional Variance (Cpv): Ratio between two times the Standard Deviation and the Range of the Scores. It measures **relative variability**

Coefficient of Empirical Proportional Variance (Cpve): Ratio between two times the Standard Deviation and the Empirical Range

Coefficient of Scale Proportional Variance (Cpvs): Ratio between two times the Standard Deviation and the Scale Range

Coefficients of Relative Variability: The different coefficients which have been developed to measure and evaluate the relative variability of a given distribution

Consistency:
The property of a given coefficient of relative variability of changing accordingly when the relative variability of a distribution is modified by means of a scale transformation . (See

Stability). It is a fundamental aspect of the *Sensibility* of a given coefficient.

Content Validity The property of a given instrument of really measuring what it intends to measure.

E

Empirical Range: Distance or difference between the maximum and minimum observed values of a distribution

Experts Panel: Research technique by which two or more judges or experts, of recognized authority, make value judgements about one or more objects or items of a given instrument

Inter-Rater Reliability: A measure of concordance among **different** judges when evaluating a set of objects or items

K

Kappa Coefficient: Coeficiente que mide la concordancia, entre o intra jueces, de los juicios valorativos acerca de un objeto o conjunto de objetos. Se define como la relación proporcional entre la concordancia ajustada por aleatoriedad y la concordancia total obervada

L

Likert Scale: Evaluating scale which uses ranks in ascending or descending order, to evaluate a determined object (item) or set of objects (items)

M

Mean: A measure of central tendency. It is the specific value around which all the other observations vary. It indicates the level of attainment, on the measuring scale, obtained by the set of the corresponding set of observations.

Intra-Rater Reliability: *A measure of concordance among the **same** judges when evaluating a set of objects or items*

Median:
A measure of central tendency. It is the specific score value above which lie 50 % of the observed cases of a distribution. It represents the level of attainment, on the measuring scale, of at least 59 % of the distribution.

Mode:
A measure of central tendency. It is the specific score value most frequently observed. It represents the level of attaimnent most common among the total number of observations.

P

Pearson Correlation:
Linear correlation between two continuos variables

R

Relative Variability:
The proportional relationship between the observed variance and

the maximum expected variance, in a given distribution.

S

Scale Range:
Distance or difference between the maximum and minimum scale values of a distribution

Stability:
*The property of a given coefficient of relative variability of staying the same when the relative variability of a distribution does not change by means of a scale transformation (See **Consistency**). It is a fundamental aspect of the general property of **Sensibility**.*

Standard Deviation:
Coefficient which measures the absolute variability of a given set of data datos. It is the average distance, in absolute value, between any of the observed values of the distribution and the arithmetic mean. In other words, it is the square root of the ratio between the sum of the squared deviations, of each of the observed values from the

.

arithmetic mean, and
the total number of
observations

Sensibility*:*
The fundamental property
of a given coefficient of
changing (consistency) or
no changing (stability)
according to variations or
no variations on the
relative variability of a
distribution.

Spearman Correlation*:*
Correlation between two
categorial variables

V

Variance*:*
The Standard Deviation
raised to the second power.
It is used for certain types
of analysis, given its
statistical properties.

.

.

INSTRUCTIONS FOR THE EXECUTION OF THE PROGRAMS AND EXERCISES IN SPSS

For books sold in Venezuela and Colombia, a CD with the programs and exercises is included. For he rest of the countries (on either the Spanish or English version), the programs and exercises can be obtained thru : **iesinfo2001@yahoo.com** or **rnieto2000@yahoo.com**.

For each of the following examples and exercises the SPSS Statistical Package (versions 6.0 thru 11.0) is required.

Put the CD (or the diskette where you have unloaded the files) in the corresponding drive. When calculating the Ccv, copy the files *.sav and *.sps in drive C and then insert a blank diskette in drive A, before running the *CVC PROG.sps.*

I.   For the calculation of Cpv (Cpve y Cpvs):

1.   Open the data file *CPV DATA.sav*.
2.   Open the syntax program *CPV PROG.sps*.
3.   Mark the whole program and run it with the command *Ctrl. + R.* , or by clicking on the *Run* option of the menu bar.
4.   Observe the output. Compare the results by opening the file *CVP OUTPUT.spo*.
5.   If you wish, print the output and/or the program of the *CPV*.
6.   To process your own data, simply substitute the data of the file *CVP DATA.sav* and run the program again.

II.   For the calculation of Ccv:

1.   Open the data file **CCV DATA.sav**.
2.   Open the syntax program **CCV PROG.sps**.
3.   Mark the whole program and run it with the command *Ctrl. + R.* , or by clicking on the *Run* option of the menu bar.
4.   Observe the output. Compare the results by opening the file **CCV OUTPUT.spo**.
5.   If you wish, print the output and/or the program of the **CCV**.
6.   To process your own data, simply substitute the data of the file **CCV DATA.sav** and run the program again.

III.   For the calculation of KAPPA:

1.   Open the data file **KAPPA DATA.sav**.
2.   Open the syntax program **KAPPA PROG.sps**.
3.   Mark the whole program and run it with the command *Ctrl. + R.* , or by clicking on the *Run* option of the menu bar.
4.   Observe the output. Compare the results by opening the file **KAPPA OUTPUT.spo**.
5.   If you wish, print the output and/or the program of the **KAPPA**.
6.   To process your own data, simply substitute the data of the file **KAPPA DATA.sav** and run the program again.

IV.   For the calculation of the Coefficients of Relative Variability:

1.   Open the data file **COEFS DATA.sav**.
2.   Open the syntax program **COEFS PROG.sps**.
3.   Mark the whole program and run it with the

.

 command *Ctrl. + R.* , or by clicking on the *Run* option of the menu bar.

4. Observe the output. Compare the results by opening the file ***COEFS OUTPUT.spo.***

5. If you wish, print the output and/or the program of the coefficients.

6. To process your own data, simply substitute the data of the file ***COEFS DATA.sav*** and run the program again.

V. For the calculation of Transformations 1 and 2:

1. Open the data file ***TRANSF 12 DATA.sav***.

2. Open the syntax program ***TRANSF 12 PROG.sps***.

3. Mark the whole program and run it with the command *Ctrl. + R.* , or by clicking on the *Run* option of the menu bar.

4. Observe the output. Compare the results by opening the file ***TRANSF 12 OUTPUT.spo.***

5. If you wish, print the output and/or the program of the ***TRANSF 1 2***.

6. To process your own data, simply substitute the data of the file ***TRANSF 12*** DATA.sav ***and run the program again.***

VI. For the calculation of Measures of Central Tendency, Variability, Empirical Range, P75, P25, Minimum and Maximum:

1. Open the data file ***COEFI 01 DATA.sav***.

2. Open the syntax program ***COEFI 01 PROG.sps***.

3. Mark the whole program and run it with the

.

    command *Ctrl. + R.* , or by clicking on the *Run*
    option of the menu bar.

4. Observe the output. Compare the results by
    opening the file ***COEFI 01 OUTPUT.spo.***

5. If you wish, print the output and/or the program
    of the ***COEFI 01.***

6. To process your own data, simply
    substitute the data of the file ***COEFI 01***
    DATA.sav and run the program again.

VII. For the calculation of the Absolute Deviations from the Mean and the Median:

1. Open the data file ***COEFI 02   DATA.sav.***

2. Open the syntax program ***COEFI 02***
    PROG.sps.

3. Mark the whole program and run it with the
    command *Ctrl. + R.* , or by clicking on the *Run*
    option of the menu bar.

4. Observe the output. Compare the results by
    opening the file ***COEFI 02   OUTPUT.spo.***

5. If you wish, print the output and/or the program
    of the ***COEFI 02.***

6. To process your own data, simply
    substitute the data of the file ***COEFI 02***
    DATA.sav ***and run the program again.***

ALL THE PROGRAMS MAY BE FREELY COPIED AND DISTRIBUTED

PLEASE ACKNOWLEDGE THE SOURCE AND THE CORRESPONDING AUTHOR (S)

IF YOU NEED SOME HELP OR ADDITIONAL INFORMATION, CONTACT THESE ELECTRONIC ADDRESSES:

iesinfo2001@yahoo.com

rnieto2000@yahoo.com